Sociable!

How Social Media is Turning Sales and Marketing Upside-down

By Shane Gibson & Stephen Jagger

Cover design: JP Valdes of JPValdes.com
Interior Design and Cover Formatting: Booksurge.com
Sociable! Logo: JP Valdes
Cartoonist: Rob Cottingham of SocialSignal.com
Editor: Greg Colombo (@gregcolombo)
Publisher: Stephen Jagger Holdings Inc.

ISBN: 1-4392-6400-7
ISBN-13: 9781439264003

"Oh, how I wish I could have read Sociable! back when I was a social media newbie. I could have prevented tons of confusion, many headaches, and loads of wasted time trying to figure it out. My advice? Read Shane and Steve's book and use it as your roadmap to taking full advantage of the tremendous sales and marketing power that social media has to offer."

Skip Anderson Founder & President,
Selling to Consumers Sales Training
sellingtoconsumers.com

"As in business and in life, actions create reputations. A brand is the conversation that users are having about a product or service. As a professional speaker, consultant and author I have been obsessed with providing the best possible staff recruiting and retention solutions thus relying solely on "word of mouth" advertising. Lately, I have felt a massive disconnect with the philosophies touted by "Social media marketing Guru's", advocating using these new mediums to market one's products or services rather than engaging with their community of users.

Happily, Shane and Stephen in their new book Sociable share how the world really works by providing their powerful insights on how organizations can actively facilitate and contribute to the online word-of-mouth conversations pertaining to their brands that will greatly impact profits."

Dr. Denis L. Cauvier best selling author of
How to Keep Staff Productive and Happy and
The ABCs of Making Money series of books
deniscauvier.com

"You guys have really nailed the critical components of using social media for business, and you've done it in language that is easily understood and enjoyable to read."

Jerry Kennedy author of
Motivation 101 and
Co-host of the *Sales Management 2.0 Podcast*
jerrykennedy.com

Sociable!
Shane
Steve
Jagger
Gibson
@ShaneGibson
@sjagger
#sociable
Social Media
Success
Thought Leadership
Market Smarter
Trust
Engagement
Dominate
Listen
Added
Value
Ubertor
Video
Profit
Action
Twitter
Giving
Sell
Blogging
SEO
Meetup
Innovate
Future Trend
ROI
#scrm
Share
Friends
Happiness
Significance
Truth
Break Rules
LinkedIn
Credit
Etiquette
Networking
Relationships
Tribes
Revenues
Beat
Win
Competition
Business Intelligence
Charity
Wallet
Links
RSS
SociableBook.com
Small Business
No Spam
Build a brand
Mind
Knowledge

Dedication

*This book is dedicated to our community;
you're the real teachers.*

Contents

Acknowledgements

Firstly we want to acknowledge our community as whole. This book is a culmination of our experience gained in interacting with our clients, friends, and community in the social media space. If we were to list everyone there would be thousands of you. Your thoughts, Twitter updates, blog comments, and feedback at Meetup events have contributed greatly to our inspiration and successes.

We also want to give special thanks to several people who helped make this book a reality:

Mr. Greg Colombo for his great feedback, editing, and ability to call BS when he saw it.

Kyle MacDonald who on top of being able to trade a red paper clip for a house was able to write a great foreword.

Stephen's wife Sarah and Shane's wife Wannapan for sacrificing date nights and supporting us through our marathon writing sessions.

Shane's son Kristian for sacrificing several perfectly good sunny days to hangout with Dad, while he worked on the book.

Our Interviewees who added depth and perspective to the book: Peter Aceto CEO of ING Direct Canada, Ian Watt of IanWatt.ca, Chris Patterson CEO of Interchanges, Scott Heiferman CEO of Meetup.com, Ryan Holmes CEO of Invoke Media, Tom Everitt of ThinkTom.com, John Chow of JohnChow.com, and Nick Usborne of NickUsborne.com.

People like Skip Anderson, Margot Jagger, Ian Watt, Bruce Jagger, Mike Jagger, Bill Gibson, Susanna Puppato, Fred Shadian, and Lynn Kitchen who waded through the draft versions of this book and gave us great insight, encouragement and feedback.

Dr. Denis Cauvier for his mentoring, guidance and feedback on the business of book publishing and professional speaking.

And of course our Twitter friends and followers you're an awesome source of insight and a great cheering committee, we hope to return the favor soon!

Foreword

Hello, and welcome to the foreword! My name is Kyle MacDonald, the author of the foreword. I sincerely hope you enjoy my pre-introduction to the book, *Sociable!* My section is short because I've spent far too many hours reading the advance copy of the book, and using the tips. I guess foreword writers aren't supposed to read the whole book, but well, I couldn't put it down.

Shane and Stephen invited me to write this foreword because I'm obviously an important qualified 'expert' in social media, and I guess they're right. But there's one thing I should probably clear up right away. I'm a digital immigrant. I'm not some eighteen-year-old wonder kid who lives and breathes social media. I did get involved in social media earlier than most; I started my first blog in 2005, which in internet terms, is just after the big bang and the formation of the universe. I started a blog at oneredpaperclip.com to help realize my goal of trading for bigger and better items, starting with a red paperclip.

I posted some ads in the barter section of Craigslist.org and looked for people to trade with. Slowly but surely, I met up with people and we made trades. I took pictures of the trades and wrote small blog posts to introduce people to the traders, to show I was legit, and to promote my next item up for trade. After several trades and several months, the blogosphere caught wind of my exploits in a big way and began to talk about my blog. A snowball effect happened where the more that people talked about it, the bigger it became, so the more people talked about it. And so forth. Next thing I knew CNN was on the phone and TV networks were sending crews to follow the trades live. It was a quite a thrill. After one year and 14 separate trades, I managed to swap from a red paperclip to a house.

That was in the old days - all I had was a blog, an email address, and a cell phone. There was no MySpace, YouTube, Facebook, Twitter, or most of the hundreds of amazing social media platforms available nowadays. There weren't even iPhones! Hard to believe, I know. Much has changed since then in the online world. Mobile technology has exploded over the last couple years, and people are more digitally intertwined than ever before. Sure, many principles of social media don't change over time: Be honest, converse as opposed to sell, and above all else, be real. But with more people becoming 'Sociable!' every day, including myself; this book is an indispensable guide to the rapidly developing realm of social media. Excuse the plagiarism, but here's a line from later on in this book I think is outrageously important, and worth repeating:

> *"It's about letting pieces of our own passions and personal identity bleed through online."*

I can honestly say that's all I understood when I started my red paperclip blog back in ye olde 2005. Be yourself, and be honest. That's it. I figured out how to construct a hodgepodge old-fashioned web presence by trial and error. I would have killed for the social media tools we have now. Well, not really, it's just a figure of speech. Luckily for you, it's quite easy to get your hands on the appropriate social media tools or to learn how to use them effectively.

The book you have in your hands will sort that all out. I learned a ton from this book. It's chock full of goodness. It's even better than this foreword. Trust me.

Have fun,

Kyle MacDonald
OneRedPaperclip.com
Author of One Red Paperclip

Introduction

The landscape of sales and marketing is in the midst of a great shift. Web strategist Jeremiah Owyang, believes that "you no longer own your brand, your customer owns your brand."[1] With the advent of the social web, often referred to as Web 2.0, the consumer can now have conversations about any brand, and those online conversations often become the brand.

Social networks and social media sites have provided the masses with tools to communicate and propagate messages rapidly, in a viral way, that at times can even overpower traditional media. A great example of this is something that occurred with CNN. They had to make several retractions because of the negative responses by internet bloggers. In April 2003, Eason Jordan, CNN's chief news executive made statements alleging that coalition troops intentionally targeting several journalists in Iraq. Soon after he retracted his statements, but the damage was already done.

Traditional media dropped the story and moved on, but for a period of two years, bloggers continued dig into the issue. He finally quit in February 2005 because he felt the issue was tarnishing CNN's credibility as a news organization.[2] It is amazing that individual bloggers are able to impact major media organizations with nothing more than their own blog writing. Now, just a few years later, CNN is integrating tools like Twitter feeds right along with their regular reporting to see what the world has to

---

1 "Strategy First on Facebook: Opportunities of a Ready-Made Marketing Platform" Webinar by Jeremiah Owyang, Jan. 10th 2008 at http://market-ingprofs.com

2 http://en.wikipedia.org/wiki/Eason_Jordan

say about a particular topic. It's a fusion of old media and Web 2.0.

We sat down in July 2008 to record our first podcast on social media together and posted it to iTunes. The topic was focused on using Twitter and Google's Grandcentral.com (now Google Voice) as sales tools. We got a lot of good feedback from the show and began to work together on joint events and lectures on social media for sales professionals and entrepreneurs.

Both of us are a bit different than most people espousing the benefits of social media marketing. Until recently, neither of us would have referred to ourselves as bloggers, podcasters, or new media consultants. When we sat down and reviewed how we had built our businesses and client rosters, we realized that the majority of it was through the use of tools like blogging, Meetups, Facebook and a variety of other web-based strategies.

Our personal meme is about being *Sociable!* Being *Sociable!* is about using social media to create real relationships that impact you, your business and your community in a positive fashion. It's about more than just the internet or social media; it's about thought leadership[3], building community, having fun, and of course being profitable.

We are sales professionals and entrepreneurs who have built our businesses using social media and social networking combined with the ability to sell and close a deal. We're business people using technology to grow our businesses, not techies trying to fit technology into a business setting. Its purpose is simple: we want to share with you "why social media is turning sales and marketing upside down" and how you can profit from it.

If you're reading this and you're a senior executive, you may be someone who has mistakenly banned people

---

3 Thought Leaders are online personalities that influence, create great content and mobilize unique groups of people or communities.

from engaging clients online, or you may have blocked tools like Facebook, Twitter, or others from your office network. People will find a way around this. Instead, you need to become proactive. Give them the technology and insight into how to use this powerful suite of business building tools and watch the results grow. *Sociable!* has been written to help you effectively wade into the sea of social media and to profit from it.

Throughout this book there will be some unfamiliar terms and tools mentioned. Don't feel like you have to read the book from front to back. If you come across a term like "Twitter" or "Meetup" and are not sure what it is, feel free to jump ahead to the section of the book that covers that topic and then come back to where you were. Most chapters were written as stand-alone modules. Read what's important to you and carry this book as a reference guide.

In Chapters One through Three, you will learn about the significant changes that are occurring in sales and marketing due to social media and hyperconnected consumers. You will also learn the role thought leadership plays in online success. Chapter Three should get you over any social media or technophobia that may be getting between you and your own success.

Chapter Four will walk you through the rules of engagement in social media. The goal of this chapter is to help you adapt to and profit from these communities while maintaining your brand integrity.

Chapters Five through Eight will help you define key social media tools like blogging, Twitter, video, LinkedIn and Facebook. Each chapter includes strategies and anecdotes on how to use these tools effectively.

Chapter Nine addresses social media etiquette, critical to your success in social media marketing. Social media is social. This means you are entering into or creating networks that have an expectation of certain behaviors. We must adopt this etiquette in order to effectively connect with these communities.

Chapter Ten is about how to deal with criticism, underhanded tactics and unruly customers, something that most companies moving into social media marketing are worried about. Most are ill equipped to deal with this new challenge. We show you how to meet these challenges head on and win.

Chapter Eleven is one of the most important chapters in the book. Building networks, blogging, or creating beautiful videos doesn't mean much unless it results in something measurable. This chapter will help you get real and get profitable with social media.

Social media success is tied to listening to your customers and monitoring discussions about your brand online. Chapter Twelve will show you what tools to use and how to get involved in the conversations about your brand online.

Finally, a great marketing idea without a solid implementation plan is usually destined to fail. Chapter Thirteen, takes all of the lessons from the book and condenses them into a simple seven-step plan for helping you launch your business into the social media space.

We hope *Sociable!* will help you expand your network, help you engage in and build community, and help you grow your business by embracing social media marketing.

Chapter One

Burn Your Business Card

Why Burn Your Business Card?

We would like you to burn your business card, not because they don't serve a great purpose but because they're a remnant of the old economy. When we talk about burning your business card, it relates to the fact that in the past we thought about mainstream marketing and advertising tools as being business cards, billboards, and expensive magazine, radio and TV ad space. In the past, corporations told you what to think about their brand, which they defined using traditional media, a one-way mode of communication. They dictated how the consumer should feel about the company.

Decades ago, all it took to own a brand was to advertise when the Jack Benny show or the Honeymooners was playing on television. All of North America was tuned into those few key programs and you could dominate the market if your brand message was delivered in their advertisement breaks. Now, in TV alone, there are hundreds of channels. In addition, the internet is consuming more and more of our media time.

There are tens of thousands of web based bloggers and podcasters, and the niches are ramifying further everyday. But it is not just single disparate voices. We also have, as Seth Godin describes them, multiple tribes being created online. These groups of individuals, who share similar interests, and are galvanized by leaders who have created a movement or single point of focus for them, forming communities of like-minded people.

Old Media is Dying

In 2009 and 2010 it is expected that between one to two out of every ten major newspapers in North America will go out of business. Most major media houses are cutting back, and we have seen bankruptcies and restructuring of newspapers and traditional media trying to protect themselves. People stop buying into companies for which they cannot measure return on investment. Being able to track how many people clicked through from a specific Google ad or Twitter link makes it much easier to gather data and project the results of an online campaign, as compared to a print media campaign.

Today, people are more likely to use Google, or some other online search tool, than the giant yellow pages directory, which is more commonly used for propping open their office door or elevating their computer monitor. It is a big shift from a decade ago, and one thing we know about change is that it is happening faster, not slower, giving us less and less time to adapt.

While writing this book, we were betting on which social network or social media platform would be acquired and assimilated, or simply made redundant by the time you read this. It's just a fact of life with the speed of evolution of internet media technologies. Daily newspapers will still exist, but most will be a smaller version of their online counterpart and most cities will not be able to support more than one daily. We don't want to come across as anti-newspaper, and we believe they continue to represent a high level of journalistic accountability. The reality, though, is that eyeballs are continuing to move online, and advertisers are following them.

Some people will respond to this change by saying, "I am just happy doing business offline." They would rather spend a lot of time and money selling on the phone or advertising and utilizing media and methods that are becoming less and less effective, instead of embracing new opportunities. The typical statement is, "I have always done it this way and it worked, why would I try something new?"

Businesses big and small should be focusing on new marketing channels. What you have always done may have worked, but even if you keep doing it a lot of those media are disappearing as their audiences move away. Century 21 Real Estate has announced that they are ceasing all TV advertising. That is a massive change in how real estate works, to have a major brand announce that they are cutting all of it. They're moving most of this budget (or whatever is left of it) online.

In short, if you are dependant on traditional media to drive traffic to your business, generate leads, or brand yourself, it's advisable to that you allot a portion of those budgets to new media and guerrilla marketing efforts. It pays not to be the last guy on a sinking ship.

Suppose information doesn't want to be free? Suppose what information really wants is to be meted out in tiny, controlled doses at an outrageously high price?

The New Consumer,
Why Traditional Media Doesn't Work

Traditional media doesn't work like it used to. This is especially true when you are targeting the younger generations.

> **Note from Shane Gibson:** "Kristian, my eight year old son, and I were watching TV when an ad came on for a new toy. Two kids were shown having fun playing with it; in fact I was already getting excited about heading down to the store and buying it for Kristian and I. Then I looked at Kristian and said 'pretty cool huh?' He wasn't buying it, the ad had not convinced him. He simply looked at me and said 'Dad, I think that is going to break.' That marketing piece that would have worked great on me as a kid, did nothing for my son."

This is what the consumers are like today. Even kids are skeptical of traditional media, but they believe what their friends say, they believe trusted referral sources. And we all know that word of mouth has always been the most powerful form of marketing.

Word of mouth now has the ability to go global, as what you say today online can grow legs and travel around the world. This is fantastic because we are seeing disruptive technologies upsetting the apple cart, causing traditional industry leaders to falter, opening opportunities for non-traditional competitors.

It's not just about economic challenges or shifts in various industries, it's that the rules of the game have changed. It is a global marketplace, which is becoming highly personal with online networking and social media marketing tools. With these tools it's possible for an individual, like a real estate agent or financial advisor, to open up shop and, by engaging consumers directly, within 18 months have a stronger brand in their immediate community than some of the big brands.

The New Consumer

In the last ten years, (Shane and Bill Gibson's company) Knowledge Brokers International "KBI," has trained over a 100,000 sales professionals across the United States, Canada, South America and South Africa. KBI has seen a significant shift in what is appropriate or what is acceptable in the marketplace. Traditionally, if you want to sell a product or service, you would put 50 people in a boiler room, give them a script and a phone, and have them indiscriminately call people. They would do the numbers and they would give everybody the same pitch.

Today, consumers want things customized, they want it authentic, they want it personalized, and they don't want sales or marketing messages shoved down their throats. They want to consume the information the way they choose to receive it. They might want it through Twitter, or through watching a video, they might want a phone call, they might want an email. But they get to choose. They insist on choosing.

Social media tools enable people to leverage themselves. Faster than any other time in history you can establish a brand and a presence thanks to social media and social networking. In a remarkably short period of time, you can develop a very strong global network of loyal followers and associates.

In June 2008 we formed a group called the Vancouver Sales Performance Meetup utilizing the Meetup.com platform. We spent $220 on targeted Facebook advertising to get the first 30 members in the group. Since then we were able to establish 500 new relationships with sales professionals in our local community in a matter of twelve months. We did this using online and offline word-of-mouth and free promotions driven by Meetup.com. Facebook and Meetup.com allowed us to rapidly take 500 relationships that were created online and solidify them offline. We get to shake hands, have a beer together, and share best practices and connect with other professionals.

In the traditional marketing sense, if we wanted to establish those relationships a decade ago, we would spend thousands of dollars on marketing, graphic design, newspaper ads and would blanket the market. We would probably also cold call, and deliver presentations and pitches. This would cost a lot more than $220 and would entail a much larger investment of time and downside risk. With our Meetup the only work we do now is show up and network, and make sure that we connect and share with the group. The success of this group is driven by the fact that these events are about community, education, and connecting.

Fire Your Marketing Department

As consultants, when we run across organizations with antiquated mentalities who want us to come in and help them fine-tune their cookie cutter, boiler room sales process, we say, "No thanks." Unless you are willing to move from being a product peddler to engaging the market like a trusted advisor, you are going to be road kill on the information highway. The consumer wants to deal with empowered individuals, every sales professional, every marketer, even your accountant has to be equipped and be a node in your marketing and sales network. If you give them the tools and direction to establish your brand, you can mobilize this untapped network, and you can fire your marketing department.

When we talk about firing your marketing department, it is not really about firing them, but shifting their focus. It's letting go of the traditional role they have played. They are no longer going to be the sponsors of the message and pushing it down, peppering the company with collateral materials that are used to sell. Instead, progressive organizations are enabling their teams with social media and social networking tools to go out and propagate the brand. They also teach their non-marketing colleagues a set of principles to grow the culture of the organization online.

Get Everyone Involved

Zappos.com is a leading online retailer that started with shoes, expanding to clothing and accessories. Everyone at Zappos is on Twitter. The Zappos website shows the staff accounts as a collective Twitter stream, so you can choose who you want to follow. Even Tony Hsieh, CEO, is on Twitter. They have heavily invested in their YouTube presence, and they allow customers to post YouTube videos right to the Zappos account. This gives them fresh live testimonials added all day long from happy customers. Their key customer service policy is about over-delivering. When they say things are going to arrive in 72 hours they sometimes arrive the next morning. This type of service stimulates online talk and testimonials.

At Zappos, branding and customer relationship development are no longer delivered in a top down approach. Tony Hsieh is sponsoring this change as he leads by example, engaging the marketplace and eliminating layers of hierarchy and class that traditionally exist in corporate environments. In the past, the CEO was untouchable. Front line people were put in little cubicles and were told what they could say and do. Now, the CEO is accessible as part of the brand and empowering his or her people with all the tools to engage in service.

These include everything from finance to social media tools. It is a flattening of the organization. It's extremely powerful, and you don't have to be a Zappos CEO to use these tools. Most of the tools these major corporations are using to become extremely successful online are free or nearly free. What you do need is a little a sense of curiosity, creativity, and a willingness to be transparent and get active and communicate to the marketplace.

Another good example of organizational flattening comes from Gillian Shaw of the Canwest News Service. Five years ago it was very difficult to track down and engage somebody in the media. Now you have people like Gillian Shaw who writes for the Vancouver Sun Newspaper and is on Twitter (@gillianshaw). You can easily create conversations with her. She talks about stories she's working on, and will engage in conversations on articles she has published. You can see Gillian communicating on Twitter with people who are throwing ideas, questions and tips her way. Gillian says it has made her life easier in sourcing stories and connecting with businesses for her popular columns and blog posts. Additionally, it's easy for the public to connect with her and have their message heard.

While writing this book we have witnessed some of the world's biggest newspapers go bankrupt or cease printing. While traditional newspapers are dying, formally trained journalists like Gillian Shaw can and will develop powerful and trusted online brands. Media will still exist, but the medium is changing.

Rapidly Leverage Your Network for Free

Historically, even if you had a large contact base, it was usually a challenge to mobilize them and get support on a project or event. It might entail dozens of phones calls, administration work and staff, and possibly costly advertising. Today you can achieve the same results faster and at a much lower cost by harnessing tools like Facebook, Meetup.com and LinkedIn.

Imagine a rookie stockbroker with a very small business network, but who happens to have been on Facebook for 2 years and developed a good sized personal network. Using Facebook, she can quickly brand herself, make new connections using tools like the "Fan Page" and Facebook events to accelerate her business growth. From her fan page she can create an event. The next step may be inviting her top 20 friends to the event along with a personal message asking each to refer or invite specific types of people from their own networks. Within a few days, and at no cost, she is able to organize an event with a group of 20-40 qualified prospects sitting in a room.

As a new stockbroker, without a tool like Facebook, it would take a significant number of cold calls and advertising dollars. Using Facebook, LinkedIn events, or Meetup. com, you are able to look at guest profiles and understand who is attending, even knowing what they do for a living, or what they ate today for breakfast. These tools can enable you, as a sales professional or entrepreneur, to organize events and gain insight into who your audience is before you meet them.

Thanks to social media you have the same ability as a large corporation to influence a broad market. Reach is no longer budget dependant.

The Reverse Drip Process

*"[traditional marketing] annoy the 90% of your audience that is not interested in your product to reach the 10% that might be" - **Chris Anderson**[4]*

Today, you have the same ability as a large corporation to influence a broad market. In the past, it was almost impossible to compete with their advertising budgets. You now have the capacity to leverage your own network. In the past, mind share was built by pushing our message out to prospects using the so-called "Drip Process," contacting the prospective client regularly with phone calls, email, lunches, personal visits, etc. The goal of a drip marketing and sales campaign is to build trust, mind share and eventually wallet share with outbound messaging. We're not arguing that this doesn't work. Indeed, it's proven to work. However, with effective planning and execution, you can create a "Reverse Drip Process" where the market comes to you instead.

After meeting with her 40 people, our rookie stockbroker doesn't have to worry as much anymore about getting them on drip email programs. Instead, she can start posting videos about her thoughts on a variety of companies, or the market in general. Over time, she can share her knowledge and demonstrate to people that she knows what she is doing. If she connects well with her initial audience of 40, and continues to deliver value to them, she can grow her network and audience base by encouraging them to bring in their own friends. She'll do this with text and video blogging. She will develop a following on Twitter. When members of her audience next meet her in person, or for the first time, they will typically already

---

4 From his podcast interview at "Managing the Grey" interviewed by C.C. Chapman http://www.managingthegray.com/2009/06/24/chris-anderson-interview/

have a shared insight and a level of trust that a traditional corporate website or brochure cannot create.

The Customers You Don't Know – *@ianwatt of IanWatt.ca*

Inman News, the leading source of independent real estate news on the web, named Ian Watt as one of the top 10 Real Estate bloggers worldwide. Ian delivers a video blog 5 days a week, predominantly discussing the Vancouver market. He forwarded an email to us that he received from a gentleman in Boston:

> *"I am a doctor, I am moving to Vancouver in a year-and-a-half, me and my wife and two kids, we are looking for a condo in Coal Harbor, I am willing to spend $1.5 million Canadian, love your website, I am looking for your opinion; is the market going down...?"*

This is a perfect example of the Reverse Drip in action. A very qualified client was watching, learning, and observing Ian. And Ian didn't know this fellow was in his audience until the man reached out with that email. Through constant communication and creating valuable content, Ian is able to attract customers that connect with his vision and personality. When he meets them, they feel like they already know him. Ian did not have to drop flyers all over the country or email a list of people that typically never get the message due to spam filters. He simply shares his knowledge and unique brand in an engaging way, through the right social media channels, and customers come to him.

Marketers historically collect info, then guard it in a locked database. The new approach is to engage this "live database" and provide the customer base with choice.

You don't have to go pushing people anymore. It's no longer about the number of messages we send out. A Reverse Drip process builds a genuine relationship. In his book *Tribes*, Seth Godin explores this concept. The term tribe refers to a group of people who are interested in what you do. This can be scary for traditional marketers. They are accustomed to building a big list of potential contacts so they can hit them all, and hope to get a 0.5% to 1% response rate. (A response could be anything from sharing your site with others, right up to making an online purchase.) The problem is that they have established credibility with 1% of their market and are just noise or, worse still, are an annoyance to the other 99%.

The traditional approach to marketing is to say, "I need to control the message. I need to build a fence, a gate, and a lock around my database. I am going to push my email at you when I want to, you are going to read the information that I want you to read, and you are going to discuss it only by submitting comments that I approve." The marketer or sales person used to control how we experienced their brands, products and services in the sales processes. This approach no longer works. People don't want to fill in their information on a site to learn about us. Your database is basically alive now. They choose whether or not they are going to learn about us. Furthermore, they choose how they are going to learn. They also choose when they will do so. It's on their timeline.

In most cases, if you have set up your blog properly, engaged in using social media tools well, and are consistent over a period of time, you are going to build a loyal following. People might change their email addresses, but they are much less likely to change the thought leaders that they are connected to. This is the real goal. Forget about being a brand leader and start thinking about being a thought leader. That's what it is about. You don't have to be the CEO of a company. You can be a brand new salesperson working for a financial institution, or a new business coach, and you can create a significant following of clients and associates in a very short time using social media and social networking tools.

Another real estate agent and client of Ubertor is Tom Everitt from ThinkTom.com. Tom shared with us just how quickly his social media activity has spun off into opportunities:

"I was introduced to video blogging and Twitter by Steve Jagger and Ubertor websites a few years ago. A television show called 'Realty TV' asked for some ideas for shows. I immediately ran to my Garagio (garage/studio) where I film my video blogs and shows. I filmed a pitch for the producers to do a story about my 'Garagio' and sent it off within an hour. They responded within 2 hours after that and the result was a 15-minute feature episode about myself and my real estate business on Realty TV. The host of the show also did an episode of my blog with me.

This kind of exposure and advertising would normally have cost tens of thousands of dollars. The result was a huge increase in visibility in the Province of British Columbia as well as nationally and internationally when I posted the episode on various websites and forums. It also led to a very substantial increase in business. The timeframe that everything happened within was literally a half a day."

Leadership at All Levels Without Permission

Frank Eliason, or as we know of him @ComcastCares, runs the Comcast customer service Twitter account and is a great social media success story. Largely due to his efforts, in 2008 Comcast was ranked by Tech Crunch as one of the top companies in the world for using social media effectively. Tech Crunch is arguably the top mainstream technology blog on the web.

Eliason was one of many people on the customer service team in the organization. And then he got on Twitter to engage Comcast customers directly. He started answering people who were having problems and complaining about Comcast in Twitter. As a group, he and his team came up with a title for Eliason, "Director of Digital Care." He has created a massive following for himself, and while he is one of many employees, he has made himself invaluable to Comcast.

When you do this, you become indispensable, a person that they cannot afford to get rid of. Who knows, they may even pay you more because you have made a name for yourself, if you can get to the point where the company needs you more than you need them.

Engagement by One of the Big Three

"Any customer can have a car painted any color that he wants so long as it is black." – **Henry Ford** (1909)

If we think about traditional top down organizations, we think of Ford. Ford talks about one of their biggest successes being centralized management and collaboration via their "One Ford Concept." Even though there are offices all around the world, they collaborate as a single unit making key decisions in one place.[5]

Ford has realized that one of the challenges they had was the online conversations people were having about their vehicles and their brand. They hired Scott Monty, now head of social media at Ford. He monitors the web all day. Monty might not describe it this way, but he actively watches Twitter, he watches the blogs. He listens to

---

5 Bill Ford (Video Interview) http://www.thefordstory.com/planandprogress/?videoId=302

conversations, and when people talk about things like why the big three US automakers are in trouble, he will get in there and talk about how Ford is different, often pointing them to check out theFordStory.com to learn what makes Ford different.

Even when someone complains about their vehicle, he is listening, engaging them, and directs them to the nearest dealership, or where to look for help. This is an example of an organization that understands the power of social media, and we believe that's the first step. What Ford needs to do now is roll this effort out to all their dealerships worldwide.

Our prophecy is that in the near future you could see most Ford dealerships throughout North America having a social media strategy in place at the dealership level and their sales team will be video blogging, and using other forms of social media. If it's not Ford then it will be someone else. But the first major auto manufacturer that does will reap the rewards.

Note From Stephen Jagger: The Ford Motor Company was an early-engaged leader online. I was invited to Ford's 100th anniversary party in Detroit. Mitch Jarvi who worked with Ubertor at the time, had created a website called FordHarley.com. He was using the Ford brand online in an unauthorized fashion. He had a lot of traffic and fans commenting about this special Ford truck called the Ford Harley.

Ford was engaged in trying to find people that supported their business, they were looking for ultra fans that had these websites, and they actually flew Mitch, Ubertor co-founder Michael Stephenson and myself to Detroit for Ford's 100th anniversary. We had VIP treatment at the whole event, along with 19 other guys that had websites and were ultra enthusiasts of Ford. Ford is good at paying attention to these things and embracing the fans. That's expensive to do. The beauty about it is that they didn't need to do it, they didn't need to fly guys into Detroit. But they did and it was powerful. It intensified loyalty to the brand.

Here's the alternative. The same cost of flying 20 guys to Detroit is probably a fraction of what a more archaic, protectionist company would spend suing them for using their brand online. This would only result in negative spin on the web, and it would cost them a lot more in the end. Hiring a team of lawyers so you can control your brand online is a lot less effective than engaging your fans and directing the conversation positively.

The Vlogger from Jersey

There are many examples of how social media tools are helping accelerate people's businesses. Gary Vaynerchuk was working in his family business in New Jersey, a relatively small wine shop doing $4 million per year in revenues. One day he picked up a video camera and in his very New Jersey style, with his accent and his enthusiasm, started to talk about wine. Gary created video blogs every day. It wasn't until the 30th week, on his 148th episode, that Gary began to get a massive response to his show at WineLibraryTV.com. The store now does over $40 million in sales. Gary has two book deals, is constantly being interviewed by TV stations across the continent, and is in high demand as a public speaker for conferences and conventions.

Not everybody loves Gary. Some people have watched his video and don't get him and have asked others, "Why do you like the guy? I don't appreciate what he has to say about wine. He isn't even using the proper terms!" What is great is that he has a very strong personality, he is consistent, and with nothing but a video camera and a website, not internet marketing, he just kept going and he slowly built his following until it exploded. The key lesson here is that you can go from being an unknown to having a strong and loyal following, without spending all the money that advertisers did, and do, using traditional marketing strategies.

Old School Sales Pro Learns New Tricks

Note from Shane Gibson: I started my career by marketing professional speaking services to conference planners and associations in the early 1990s. When I first started, I wasn't speaking at conferences, but I was working in my family business, booking speakers for conferences. At that time, if I wanted to book a speaker 20 times a year, I would have to be in the office all day, burning up the phone calling lists of conference organizers.

I would get on the phone, and "hammer" it. Once someone was interested, I would fax them a one or two sheeter on what we offered then I would follow up. If they were qualified, I would send out a very expensive package, which included a CD, a full color brochure, a stack of photocopied reference letters, and pay to courier it to them. That whole process just to pitch the client not only took a long time, it was also quite expensive. To get 20 deals I would have to send out at least 100 packages, at considerable cost.

In 2001, my business was getting about 5% of its business coming from our websites, while the rest was cold calling and word of mouth. Fast-forward to 2009 and 80% of revenues generated are from web based and social media leads.

There has been a shift in web literacy and in decision-making power in the marketplace. In the past, when people were researching who to hire for a conference speaker, it was Betty, the 60-year-old personal assistant who has been working at XYZ company for a few decades who was in charge of that. Betty has retired in the last three years, and along comes Paul or Sarah. They are 20 to 30 years old, are university educated, and they are digital natives. They were born with a computer in their hand. They don't go to the Yellow Pages when they need a new product or service. They research it online; trusting in feedback received via social media and in the top search engine results.

A lot of these tools are going to change. We are going to talk about Twitter, Facebook, Viddler among others, and how to best utilize them, but at the end of the day those tools might change. Twitter could go out of business or be bought by somebody else. Nonetheless, hang on to the principles in this book on how to engage people, to perpetuate your brand, and we believe that you can be a household name in the market niche that you want to dominate.

Chapter Two

Digital Citizens and Levels of Engagement

The Digital Natives Are Restless

Mark Prensky, author of *Digital Game-Based Learning*[6], coined the terms "Digital Native" and "Digital Immigrant" to describe two distinct groups of people involved in technology. The digital immigrant is anyone born in 1979 or earlier. These people tend to look at technology as a utility to get something done, as something separate from them.

Most people born after 1980 in western countries would be digital natives. They were born with a PDA or cell phone strapped to their hand. Technology is second nature to them. It is part of their culture, it's not an add-on. While there is much criticism of this demographic and their work ethic, they are extremely adept at simultaneously managing multiple tools and channels of communication. They may say, or think, something like, "Who cares if I pay attention as long as I get the work done, and by the way I'm going to socialize online while I'm working."

While attending a recent networking event for high tech professionals in Vancouver, BC, put on by 6S Marketing called Ideas on Tap, these two demographic groups became quite obvious. One group networked with a drink and business cards, the other with a drink and an iPhone.

6 Digital Game Based Learning, by Mark Prensky - McGraw Hill, 2001

The iPhone crowd posted pictures, had conversations with other event attendees online, and shared Twitter IDs. Some using the "Bump" application simply bumped their iPhones together to exchange contact details instantaneously. They were completely content with talking to one another as they engaged each other online. They didn't have to wait until the next day to draft an email and send it out to everyone they had just met. They were already instantly connected, and most likely had read each other's blogs, watched each other's YouTube channel and possibly commented on their respective Twitter streams by the next day. "Business cards, what are those?"

The Social Media Matrix and Thought Leadership

We sat down and looked at several stages of social engagement online and put together the Social Media Matrix. We looked at different types of participants in social media and the benefits for those involved.

We initially found three types: the Thought Leaders, the Engaged Participants, and the Disengaged. Later we realized that there was, unfortunately, a fourth group, which we have labeled Old World Spam Artists. Within the Engaged participant category we have identified 3 levels of engagement.

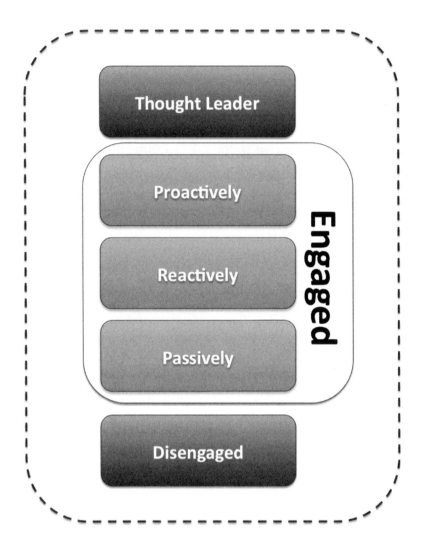

Participant Levels of Engagement

The Old World Spam Artist

One group that isn't included in the Social Media Matrix are the spam artists, but they are alive and well in almost every nook and cranny of the internet. These people (and companies) think of Twitter and Facebook as free advertising. Most of their messages are about themselves.

They may have hundreds of people connected to them, but the only time they contact them is to pitch a product or service, or to let them know how great their company is. Spam and flooding people with "Me" focused messages is not social media. The communication needs to be both ways; it must be a dialogue.

These types of marketers need to shift their focus, start sharing, and start promoting other people's vision and passions. Being successful in social media and social networking is about building community. If you feel you fall into The Old World Spam Artists category you need to begin to focus on building relationships, community and credibility. The money will follow.

Your strategy needs to encompass everyone in the Social Media Matrix

All of these groups of people, except the disengaged, are important parts of your social media strategy as a sales professional. You need to put more than your big toe in the water. If you want to profit from social media and social networking, you have to be a thought leader. You have to be the one creating content, developing blogs, getting involved in social networks or even creating your own social networks to harness the power of the individuals who are interested in what you have to talk about and your niche.

Disengaged Participants

A big part of the demographic right now isn't involved in any type or form of social networking or social media. In fact many of them only know how to use Microsoft Office. Typically these people are in the early Baby Boomer demographic. These people are "Digital Immigrants" and they're still coming online by the thousands. They're also most likely to get duped by an internet chain letter hoax. Many of them have great offline networking skills and business acumen, and if they invested in their computer literacy could be a strong force on the web.

Passively Engaged Participants

There are three levels of positive engagement for participants. The lowest rung is a passive participant. This is the reader of blogs, the viewer or listener of podcasts. This is someone who visits websites, but who does not actively engage. This person tends to consume but not share resources or opinions. They are passively engaged. They absorb the information, they form opinions, but they don't get involved in the conversation. They may be influenced, but are not influencers. They will still buy products and services online, and even respond to a retailer's website by visiting a store in person, but there is rarely an online spin-off or multiplier effect attributed to them enjoying what they have seen or experienced. They tend to stick to mainstream portals or news sites and rarely venture into niche sites or personal blogs for information.

Reactively Engaged Participants

The next group is what we call reactive participants. These are the people who get involved, yet could still be considered window shoppers. They are involved in social networks, they put up a profile, but you wouldn't find them creating a dialogue. They will add friends and they may even make the odd comment, but they are careful and infrequent with their engagement.

Don't worry if you're in this category. It's not necessarily a bad place to start. Most corporate types have been taught to manage their image and keep a distance from people. This is often where people start off in the social space. The key to profiting and growing a network is taking the next step and becoming proactively engaged.

Proactively Engaged Participants

This is where we move beyond being responsive to proactive. These are the people who get on your website and engage. They ask you questions, they comment, these are the ones who forward your videos to their friends, these are the ones who do a video response to your video online, they are on Twitter responding to your comments, engaging you, forwarding your information. They are connectors as Malcolm Gladwell calls them in his book "The Tipping Point."

To Win in Social Media You Want to Be A Thought Leader

Thought Leaders fall into a larger group, according to Forrester Research, called Creators. Depending upon the sector, creators only make up between 11% and 20% of those people involved in social networking and social media.[7] They are a minority within the creator demographic, but Thought Leaders are the ones who harness the power of the crowd. They harness the power of social media and social networking, they direct thoughts, and they set the pace for social media etiquette in the marketplace. Depending on which space they occupy, from a commercial perspective, from a sales and marketing perspective, they can also profit the most. Thought Leaders are also the least susceptible to having negative comments about their brand online get out of control or impact them in negative ways, because of their level of influence online.

---

7 http://www.forrester.com/Groundswell/profile_tool.html

It is important to note that, in business, simply creating content by publishing blogs, videos or participating or starting discussions doesn't make you a thought leader. For the purpose of building trust and credibility, creating a YouTube video of your best friend opening a beer bottle with his teeth may get you a lot of video views, but if you're not selling beer or dental repair, it probably is not going to help your brand. Leadership is about making a positive impact, a movement, providing a platform or guidance to others in your field of expertise and passion.

"If you think you're a leader and no one is following you, you're actually just going for a walk." – **author unknown**

John Maxwell, author of the ground-breaking book *Developing the Leader Within You*, provides a definition of leadership in one word: influence. A thought leader in the social media space is measured by their level of influence. Online we can boil it down to creating action within the community you are connected to and beyond. These actions can include:

1. Creating messages and content that others pass on
2. Providing mentorship or content that helps people grow personally
3. Helping other people become successful
4. Changing or molding other peoples views about a product, person, industry, company, political outlook or even a place
5. Solving other people's problems
6. Making people laugh or creating joy
7. Causing people to experience strong emotions or create a desire to change

8. Listening to and empathizing with others thus causing a positive reaction or increased brand equity
9. Effectively selling or promoting a product, service or event
10. Getting people to take political action by voting, protesting, blogging or other forms of voicing opinions

One important thing to note is a lot of the things listed above are also characteristics of people who are great members of a community, but this is not enough. The reality is if you sound like everyone else you're not a thought leader. You may be a promoter of ideas, a content sharing channel, but not a thought leader. Thought leadership is about creating original distinct content that creates results like the ones listed above.

If You Sound Like Everyone Else, You're Not a Thought Leader

It is important when you get into the social space that you not sound like everyone else. If you are trying to offend no one, and appeal to everyone, you are going to lose. You will be drowned out by the noise online. It may seem that the safe way to get involved is to not make anybody mad, not be aggressive in any way. It is actually the unsafe path, because it turns into a waste of your time, as there is no benefit for you at all if you are not being noticed. It is better to be having your opinions and your thoughts published, because people will notice you and pick up on what you do. That is how you create the conversation, create followers, and create business.

When we look at Ian Watt and his blog, some of his video blog entries push the envelope of acceptability to some, but we still respect him because he draws a line in the sand. Ian effectively says to us, "This is who I am, this is my brand, these are the type of customers I want to attract" and he has well above average web traffic in comparison to other local real estate agents.

We see other real estate agents that have been around just as long, who also have blogs, but they put up the same information as all their peers. They have the same opinions, endorse the same speeches by local government people on where the economy is heading, and they promote the same development projects. Ian, on the other hand, is often a bold contrarian and he gets noticed because of it. The reality is that people who sound like everyone else are not building a distinctive brand, because they haven't established a true identity. It isn't about not offending people and controlling opinions; it is actually about making sure you stand out from the crowd.

You are not trying to lead the whole web. Your goal is to build a strong group of people who are connected to you. We don't like to call them followers. We like to use the term participants, indicating that the people connecting to you are a part of something bigger. The key is to develop a strong group of participants who are in line with your values and what you believe in passionately. The more passionate and polarized you can be, often the more effective you can be.

How to Influence Thought Leaders

"Influentials are on average about twice as likely as the average American to be sought out for advice and opinion" – **Ed Keller and Jon Berry** authors of *The Influentials*

Social media and social networking are great tools and they do give you the capacity to build a following. But if you want to accelerate and multiply your following and get your message out into the marketplace in a very viral way, then you want to connect to other networks, and get endorsements from other major thought leaders.

There is so much information for people to sift through and determine its value that people today are overwhelmed. So they often turn to thought leaders, or "Influentials" for guidance. Most people will go to a thought leader on a specific topic to get advice or access information through their blog, Twitter stream or other publishing platforms. When you want to get the word out quickly, trying to directly influence people that you have recently connected with online can be tough. Often it is easier to invest time and resources in establishing rapport with the thought leaders that influence these people.

Note From Shane Gibson: Prior to an event I was to do for the Vancouver Board of Trade I was informed that the expected attendance numbers were down a little bit, as there were several major board functions happening that month. So, a few weeks before my event, instead of going the traditional route of more marketing, more emails to the same groups, the Board of Trade and I reached out to other thought leaders with their own followings on the internet. These were people with whom we had already established strong relationships with over the previous year.

We connected with people with like Tom Everitt from thinktom.com, who had large audiences for his video blogs, and whose demographic was concentrated in the immediate area where the seminar was being held. Tom had me on as a guest on his program, talking about the upcoming seminar as it might be of interest to his own constituency.

I also connected through Twitter to numerous other thought leaders who passed messages on about the event. Within a few days, numbers were running at a profitable level. This all had to do with connecting with other thought leaders and giving them content and value for their networks, and where they don't feel like they are giving a pitch. I was introduced as another thought leader into their groups and brought something of value. In this case it was tips and processes for selling and succeeding in tough economic times. In doing so, all parties won. Each thought leader received new content that helped their respective communities. And the Board of Trade and I were able to leverage influence and reach a wider potential audience base by connecting through trusted leaders in the online community.

Be creative and do what it takes

Note From Stephen Jagger: A while back I noticed that Gary Vaynerchuk of Wine Library TV was about to be in Seattle as part of his book tour throughout the United States. I created a Reachd. com training event in Seattle, normally held in Vancouver, around the date that Gary was to be there. I then asked Gary if he would come by before his book signing to speak briefly about his experience with online video.

On the basis of that first encounter, I now have a great relationship with Gary and his team. A year later, Gary recorded a video testimonial about Reachd.com and our training sessions. It's great to have an endorsement from Gary, a sensation who receives 80,000 to a 100,000 viewers for each of his videos.

Cool or Passion Filled Information Gets Shared

When you're reaching out to thought leaders in the social space you need to tap into their motivations. Many that have become hubs or key connectors in their networks have done so by providing cutting edge, unique or exciting and entertaining information and opportunities to those they are connected to.

Things that can get you noticed by thought leaders could include:

1. First access to new technology
2. News or insight that is not yet publicly available
3. Opportunities to review products or services before other people
4. Exclusive opportunities they can bring to their network to add value
5. Information or opportunities that would support their values or mission
6. Cutting edge studies or stats on areas that are of interest to them or their community
7. Opportunities for them to be profiled on your blog, podcast, or show
8. Opportunities for them to appear in your book, magazine or whitepaper
9. Connecting them with another thought leader in your network

Make it Easy for Them to Promote You

Big online influencers are busy. They're more inundated with information than those who seek their insight and leadership. If you want them to share your information, you'll need to provide it in multiple formats that can be easily dispensed.

Don't make them dig through multiple pages on your blog or website for information. If it's a video you want them to distribute to their community, make sure it's easy to cut-and-paste into their blog or site. If it's a white paper you want them to read and share, make sure the file size is small and easy to download, and that it's in a format that is current and compatible with most computers.

The key message here is make it easy for them to digest and evaluate your information by providing it in multiple digital formats that are easy to use and share with others. Don't make thought leaders do the mundane work you should have done. The harder it is for your information to be accessed or shared the less likely it is for your message to spread virally on the web and beyond.

Build Rapport in Person with Thought Leaders

One of the most effective ways to establish relationships with people is to take it off-line. In other words, meet them face-to-face if at all possible. Hosting a "beer for tech bloggers" event in your community if you want to build rapport with that sector could help you achieve in one night what it would take a year to do online.

If there's a well-known author who has a large online following that corresponds to your target market, make sure you attend their next seminar when they are in town. Introducing yourself and chatting for a few minutes after the session will make your future online interactions more valuable to them, and in most cases they will have a more personal and emotional connection to your online identity.

Although this book is about being sociable online, we cannot discount the value of a one on one meeting to get things rolling. In fact, being Sociable! is about building relationships using all forms of interaction and influence.

Chapter Three

Social Media Phobia

"Change happens in an instant, it just takes us a while to adjust" - **Anthony Robbins**

Organizations that embrace change and use it to their advantage reap the greatest rewards. Hockey legend Wayne Gretzky often said that he didn't go where the puck was; he went where it was going to be. This is what profiting from new trends, or shifts in technology, is all about.

Many people who are successful today adjusted or even preempted these shifts in technology. Apple's iTunes store is a good example of this. While the recording industry was fighting online music distribution Apple capitalized on it. Social media phobia is going to be many organizations' biggest block in profiting from the social web.

A phobia is an irrational fear, an anxiety built around an untruth, neuroticism or in some cases a traumatic past event. There is a fear of losing control. Consider how much the traditional record labels have suffered because of their fear of digital distribution of music. The harder they fight it, the harder they try to control the content, the more creative people become online through social networks and other types of distribution systems to bypass whatever anti-piracy restrictions the industry puts into place. The music recording industry largely has not embraced new media to find creative ways to generate revenues. Rather, they have either ignored it, or tried to litigate instead of innovate.

Many organizations are having the same reaction to social media as record labels had to the web. They're pulling back, trying to control or stamp out that which they do not understand.

> *"The advances in technology impact everyone, and we all must adapt... They [the industry] have to maximize their income from concerts and merchandise. "* – **Chris Anderson** from *Free the Future of a Radical Price*

The reality is that the music industry as a whole is not dying, the traditional record label is, because they've failed to adapt. In 2008 iTunes added 4 million new tracks to their library[8], and free music has also become a big contributor to the highly lucrative $2 billion concert industry.

Fear of No ROI

The common theme is loss of control or uncertain return on investment. Addressing return on investment is important. It's also important to note that with new media and technology those who wait to see certain proof of ROI rarely are the ones that reap the greatest benefit. During the Dotcom boom of the late 1990s most business people were not building websites or worrying about search engine marketing for the same reasons listed above. They said things like:

> "My customers aren't on the internet."
> "There's no proven return on investment."
> "It's for the younger generation."
> "We are already successful using print advertising."

---

8   Free the Future of a Radical Price, by Chris Anderson, page 155

"People will not buy books online."
... And the list goes on.

There is a real benefit to engaging in this medium sooner than later. Yet valid questions do arise: Is it worthwhile? Is my target market using this medium? Is there an immediate ROI?

iTunes is the biggest retailer of music in North America, surpassing even Wal-Mart. Amazon is the biggest book retailer on the planet. CreateSpace, an Amazon subsidiary, printed this book. Amazon and Apple are both great examples of companies that engaged in online marketing well before there was significant proof that they would succeed. The same is about to hold true for those now involved in Social Media. Some industries already have some metrics, such as the wine industry with new players emerging with the likes of Gary Vaynerchuk, and their success stories verify that this medium works. Other industries and geographic regions are truly virgin territory.

If I am Using Social Media Who is my Audience?

As an early adopter social media may not help you hit a home run right away within your marketplace. It is important to ask if your market is ready for you. However, do you want to wait until the market is ready until you decide to become a master of the art of social media? When the day comes that your competitors are finally rushing online in a panic trying to figure it out, you can be seen as a leader. We can look at Twitter and assume that it is only being used by a fringe group of innovators and geeks. This is far from the truth.

According to quantcast.com, as of June 2009 30% of Twitter users were between the ages of 35 and 49 years old. The largest percentage, 49%, is the 18 to 35 year old market. While 28% of Twitter users earn between $30,000 and $60,000 a year, 25% of Twitter users earn $60,000 to $100,000 a year and 27% earn over a $100,000 a year. That is a pretty rich target environment. 46% are college graduates, with 17% being grad school graduates, so this is a highly lucrative group of individuals who are typically in middle to upper management in most industries. This is not a demographic we can afford to ignore.

The other argument is that your existing target market isn't using social media. If so, is that the market you want to stay with?

People put more merit in word of mouth endorsements, and in the comments of friends, rather than the traditional advertisements pushed at them. Even if you are still using traditional media, we believe you will benefit by engaging in this lightening fast method of developing more word of mouth. The biggest failure you can have is simply not trying, pretending that the phenomenon of social media is not happening.

Phobia of social media is often a fear of learning something new. It is a fear of looking like we don't know what we are doing, being ineffective or appearing ignorant or behind the times. Most people, however, are forgiving. For example, if you travel abroad and try to speak a foreign language, the locals don't generally laugh at your attempts. Instead, you will usually find that they encourage you, seeing that you are trying. The online community is very much like that, as well. So many people are adapting to this new technology that right now is a great time to get online begin to learn along with them. There are great online and local community support networks committed to helping entrepreneurs, business owners and sales executives learn how to use these tools effectively.

Rational Fears

There are some valid fears around security. You may not want to reveal your address or too many other personal details better kept private, but you might offer your opinion on some subject, share a few of your favorite quotes and let people know when you update your blog. You can participate on a safe level.

Cameras that automatically tag your photos with geo-data can allow online viewers to pinpoint where you've taken the photos, whether that be on a vacation or in your own home, which could show off a nice stereo, pricey plasma TV, or artwork ripe for thieving. Turning off the geo-tagging option on your camera or smart phone, and posting holiday pictures after you get home can combat this.

Another realistic fear that you should have as a company owner or sales manager is wasted time and resources from blindly promoting the use of social media marketing in your organization. One your staff will be some who are tech savvy and have a sense of productive social activities and etiquette, and there will be others who aren't equipped to use the tools immediately. This doesn't mean we shut them out or worry about them embarrassing us online. What it means is that you need education or a coaching plan to get them up to speed, and an implementation strategy when you are ready to roll it out. It's the same as sitting a brand new sales person on the phone without training, or letting an intern plan next year's entire marketing strategy. The results would be underwhelming. This is not a social media issue, it's a training issue.

The Fear of Losing Control

Many people born in an earlier era where corporate mandates were handed down and executed without question are struggling with the new lightening fast and collaborative workplace. They're also struggling with the highly open and publicly personal lives of Generation Y and many of those in Generation X as well. The new breeds of consumer and worker are more connected, more open about how they are feeling and publicly sharing what they do and do not like. Many of these people have found their voice online and are connected to several networks simultaneously using computers and smartphones. When they arrive at work they behave much the same. There is opportunity in having people work for you that are wired to connect. This new breed of worker is already networking and using social media during work hours. They love to do it. All we have to do is give them some direction and incentive to do it for your brand.

> *"Some companies are scared to let their employees loose on the web. The web is about connecting people to other people who share common interest. The web will take the control whether you like it or not. Having a strategy to embrace it is the best option"* – **Nick Usborne** (NickUsborne.com)

Having a small group of people controlling a company's marketing and messaging is a business management model whose time has passed. Corporations today have to do more with less. We want to make everybody in the organization a marketing node directed by a set of social media guidelines that are positive, create transparency and help staff operate within a set of principles. Develop your own corporate social media etiquette for your people to follow. This is not about demanding control, it is about extending and expanding your community influence.

The person or people making the rules should understand what social media does, how it works and what the benefits are. It is very difficult to write rules or corporate policy about a tool if you don't understand how it works. The first step in alleviating the fear is to get to know the tools well.

If you feel disorientated and lost it's probably a good thing

Change, new technologies, and different processes for marketing and sales will often make us feel disorientated or lost. This is natural, especially because social media tools are so new. We are all social media amateurs. We learned so much after we wrote the first draft of this book that we had to go back and change entire sections. This wasn't a failure, it was a correction and an adaptation based upon a rapidly changing landscape.

The best way to overcome social media phobia is to give yourself and your organization permission to experiment, learn and adapt. It is better to have a phobia of spending big dollars on traditional marketing strategies and PR that could have been replaced with free or nearly free social media tools and strategies.

In Summary:

1. There are new media available to audiences, consumers and advertisers which if embraced can create
   win/win dialogue, communities and connections.
2. People and companies are migrating their attention and dollars to the social media space.
3. Sticking with "tried and true" old systems and
   media may work for a while but its effectiveness is
   diminishing.
4. If your business doesn't embrace the new media,
   you are missing opportunities for your business,
   and the new and especially young audiences may
   miss your messages altogether.
5. Resisting this shift could turn your organization
   into your industry's equivalent of the archaic recording companies that are holding onto an old
   method of engagement and doing business.

Chapter Four

The Rules of Engagement for Social Media And Social Networking

Before we jump into using any online tool it is vital that that we first understand the rules of engagement. It would be like hopping in a car before learning the rules of the road. We have compiled seven key rules of engagement that we have developed based upon our own personal successes and mistakes as well as through observing key thought leaders and influencers online.

Rule #1 Stop Pitching and Start Connecting

When you enter into or join a social media community it is just that, a community. People use these tools because it allows them to have very personal, transparent connections and relationships with other people. As a marketer or sales person it's important that we understand this when we engage people.

Not unlike someone trying to sell insurance at a dinner party, many will shun the social media marketer that solely talks about their product and does not add value. With any type of networking we need to have a long-term brand building and relationship building focus. If you are there for the short transaction, you are going to be on peoples' blacklist very, very quickly. In using social media as part of our marketing arsenal, we want to move from pitch artists and order takers to trusted advisors. Networking, online or offline is not about generating referrals so much as it is about becoming referable.

We have seen many people begin using online tools, whether it is blogging, podcasting, Twitter, or Facebook, and quickly do their brand a disservice. These tools provide a quick way to show people what you are about, for better or for worse. An insincere pitch artist is going to be exposed sooner online than offline, and to a potentially much wider audience. Worse, often what we publish online is stored in multiple places on the internet, forever.

You can visit a person's corporate blog and very quickly determine whether or not they get the concept of connecting versus pitching. Some of the indicators that they are being unsociable are if they:

- ✓ are writing mostly about themselves
- ✓ are controlling comments
- ✓ are not open to negative criticism
- ✓ are not talking about their competitors
- ✓ are only talking about what they are selling,

Some indicators that someone is an adept Sociable Media Marketer are:

- ✓ They are writing their blog themselves, not using ghost writers
- ✓ They write like it is a conversation with a friend
- ✓ If they are willing to engage everyone on their blog, even competitors or critics
- ✓ If they create a positive conversation, maybe even spend some time making comments on other peoples' sites
- ✓ If they allow comments on their blog
- ✓ They are authentic

This positive behavior implies that they are willing to engage and become what we refer to as a thought leader. This behavior is also building trust for their brand. People begin to see you and your company as authentic when you open up to this type of dialogue.

Rule #2 Doers Win in the game of Social Media

Successful marketers and salespeople who use the web well realize very quickly that there is no such thing as "testing if social media works." There is no such thing as testing. Life is an experiment, you can't do it half-heartedly. People will say, "Oh, I joined Twitter" or "I joined Facebook" or "I've started a blog," and you go to their blog and they have made two entries in the last four months, or they have made two entries on Twitter, they have added a bunch of people to Facebook, but they have hidden their identity, their photos, what they do for their living, and it is all controlled. This is not going to build a following of any kind.

You may initially test the waters using various media to see which gives you the best ROI. Even in that instance you still have to be fully involved in the conversation. It is a waste of your time and it is a waste of your audience's time, and it is not going to help your brand. It says, "I don't believe in this," or worse, "I am afraid." The winning principle is jump head first into the deep end of the pool, and don't be afraid. You must be willing to get messy, risk making a few errors, and promote your brand. It is better to be too transparent than to be veiled, contrived or controlled, as people will perceive that you are inauthentic.

Being online is about managing your online reputation. You can't do that by putting your big toe in the water. It is like saying I decided I am no longer going to answer my phone. Well, you know what? That is not going to work, and neither is turning off the internet and hoping it is not there. (More on this later, as Chapter Twelve is devoted to online reputation management.)

The key to doing is not just responding to or distributing interesting content, it's about becoming a thought leader. This is your main goal when creating content or building communities online.

Rule #3 It's Not About You

When people follow your messages, watch your videos or read your blog, it's about them. They're looking for personal insight, motivation, affirmation, relationships, and a broad range of other benefits and outcomes for themselves. They're not connecting with you for your benefit. Your social media and social networking strategy needs to be based on the same strategy Darcy Rezac talks about in his book *Work the Pond!* According to Darcy and co-authors Gayle Hallgren-Rezac and Judy Thomson, when you go to a networking event, the first time you meet somebody, the first question that should be on the top of your mind is, "How can I help this person?"

In social networking and social media, you need to ask yourself the same question, "How can I help my participants?" The more people you help, the more they are going to move from being passive to proactive. Your proactive participants are your fans and advocates. Advocates are the clients or people who have experienced your business or service and want to talk about you. You couldn't shut them up even if you paid them. If someone has negative things to say about you online, you don't have to worry about responding to them on your blog, because your advocates will do it for you.

Engaged Participants Will Help your Brand

Note From Stephen Jagger: Ubertor, a real estate software company I founded with Michael Stephenson, hosts and supports thousands of realty related websites.   Ubertor had a competitor spamming the client base. Having a competitor approach or spam your clients is bad enough, but some of the information included in the emails was either incomplete or just plain inaccurate.   As a company Ubertor didn't respond, and just continued to conduct business as usual. We just worked hard to improve the product and service offerings and engage our clients. Then something interesting occurred. A small group of thought leaders and actively engaged participants in the industry responded to the spam emails publicly via video, each talking about this company's behavior online and asking them to stop the spam. It was a very powerful way to do it, because it was not Ubertor asking the competitor to stop, it was key participants in the community. It was the customer saying, "Stop doing this, it is annoying. I don't need your spam." Ubertor did not ask these real estate agents to step in.   It went to show that we don't control our own brand. Our customers do, and in this case they were defending it.

These advocates had a sense of ownership in the Ubertor technology. They were happy customers, blogging online and talking about it offline, because it helped their business. When somebody stepped on Ubertor's toes, we didn't have to worry about running an ad in the *New York Times* to counter his competitor's comments, we didn't have to call a lawyer to get them to stop. They were shamed on-line and that is so much more powerful and more genuine than the company or employees respond-ing to it. The key lesson here is that authentic com-munity building trumps spam and push media.

Rule # 4 Be Fearless In Your Contribution to Your Community

"There is a time to take counsel of your fears, and there is a time to never listen to your fear." - **George S. Patton**

Being fearless is about contributing and connecting. It's about taking a risk by asserting and exposing ourselves online, leaving our thoughts, our unique brand personal-ity out there for others to observe, hopefully admire, and possibly criticize.

An example of being fearless would be to invite com-petitors in your industry to an online forum to help your collective clients. This could come in the form of an in-dustry wiki, a LinkedIn group, a Facebook group or even an offline Meetup.com function.

Get engaged versus trying to control your content, your intellectual property.

Note From Shane Gibson: I have several hours of podcasts and free information on my blog and podcast sites. With every new podcast I upload, the blog's web traffic increases and I'm increasingly getting more business from all around the world. People are booking me to speak at seminars, for training, and consultation. Our goal in selling is to create an environment where an act of faith can take place, and that act of faith is based upon credibility and trust. The more you help and contribute, the more you become a known individual, the larger that trust becomes. I give away more content than most people in my industry have to offer, yet it's that fearless abundant giving that has grown my client base.

You Had Me From Hello

Jeff Booth, CEO of BuildDirect.com, first started off as a client of KBI and Reachd then later became a good friend. The relationship started a little differently than a typical "prospect vs. salesperson" scenario. Jeff was looking at a competitor of Knowledge Brokers to help fine tune and improve BuildDirect's sales process. This competitor was better known yet BuildDirect decided within the first meeting to hire KBI instead. Jeff later told us that by the time he called Shane, he had already decided he was going work with KBI. Jeff had listened to Shane's podcasts, read his blog and opinions, and then contacted a few KBI clients he was familiar with in his personal and business networks as references.

Jeff once joked with Shane saying, "You had me from Hello!" What he was talking about is that there was no fear of saying yes, there was no unknown. He already knew the way Shane thought, and he knew some KBI methodologies. KBI gives away more online content than most people would say you should. It created an ultimate amount of trust and it showed that, "Hey! These guys are not afraid, they are very confident, they have a lot to offer." Being transparent and active, being a thought leader, can take all the fear out of saying yes.

By creating a public profile for your company, or your own personality, you are proving accessible to potential and existing clients. You reduce barriers. If they want to listen to your opinions, they can do that. If they want to watch you speaking, they can do that. They can read about you and your blog. The consumer or potential customer can now experience and learn about you in the medium they want, and in the timeframe they want. As in the previous chapter when we talked about Ian Watt and his client from Boston, by the time they are emailing you or calling you they already are 3/4 through the sales process. Instead of you putting people on a drip email and phone program, the customer is choosing to follow you.

It's intimidating to think that you don't know who is actually following you. It is a different way of communicating to your potential clients, because they are watching and waiting for a good time in their business to make that jump. When they call they may have been watching you for six months. Instead of worrying about collecting names, worry about creating great content, messages, and contributions. You will have a bigger community than you'll ever need to propagate your message or your business.

Rule #5 Don't Be a Social Spammer - Get Involved

Our Sales Performance Meetup group is made up of 500 sales professionals that get together and share best practices once a month. Once or twice a month we have somebody contact us from another city, 1000 miles or more away, wanting access to our group, they are looking for recruits or to sell their sales software perhaps. Usually this individual joins the group, adds us to their Facebook contacts, and the first thing they say is not, "How can I help?" It is, "Dear Shane and Steve, I would like to paste this information on these job opportunities, leverage your network and the relationships you have built to see if I can recruit some of these people for my organization."

Now, at first glance you might think, "Well, this is bringing in opportunity and value to the members." Here is why we won't do it for them. First, we don't know who they are. We don't know anything about their brand, there is no trust established. Next, they haven't asked, "How can I help you?" They haven't talked about how they might be able to contribute to the organization. They probably haven't even gone onto our blog and made a comment. They may have added us to a social network, and while we are just beginning to establish trust, they have gone right from "Hello!" to "Will you marry me?" We don't even know who they are or what we stand for.

Why would we refer them when we have four recruitment companies that either attend the Meetup or are actively engaging our members online? There is a relationship there. At the end of the day, **it is not about getting referrals; it is about becoming referable.**

Getting Involved

Instead, here is what one of these recruiters could have done. Get involved, offer some advice or lend a helping hand. Provide a white paper that our members would be interested in. The question should be, "How could I as a recruiter go from looking like a pitch artist, and someone who is basically trying to scoop other people's employees out of a network, to being seen as a resource and a thought leader?" This is all about negative vs. positive prospecting or networking. The people who are spamming or cold contacting us are being proactive, but in an archaic way that does not add value.

The new rule is to become referable. Be a trusted resource. Become a thought leader. Ask, "How can I help you?"

We are members of the Vancouver Board of Trade. Many people that become members pay for their one-year membership attend a few events then say, "Look, I have met nobody important and I don't want to go anymore events. It is a waste of time." But the questions they should be asking themselves are "Have I been important to other people? How have I added value?" Those people who contribute the most to the communities they are involved in reap the most rewards. Maybe not immediately, and they may also be perceived as doing a whole lot of work and giving stuff away for free, but at the end of the day, they are the ones with the biggest network and the most referrals and the trusted brands.

Rule #6 Be Authentic

We like to look at the process of creating a Reverse Drip as reputation management. Some refer to it as branding. In fact, we have been to a few seminars recently where bloggers talk about building your online brand and these same people are careful about what they reveal online. They even allude to the fact that online and in public they are a very different person than they are at home or with their friends. We disagree with this approach. If you are not a nice person, then maybe you should work on that first, before you start creating a "nice person" brand in the community.

The difference between using reputation management to build a trusted brand and creating a brand is it is leadership driven authenticity, and being a thought leader versus being a spin-doctor in creating an image online. It is exhausting to try to be someone you are not. Instead, work on being a true leader. This type of approach tends to attract an equally authentic and loyal group of participants. If you want to attract better clients, be a better leader, improve on your contribution to the community.

Social media and networking is more personal than traditional marketing or sales. It's about letting pieces of our own passions and personal identity bleed through online. This enables you to have conversations with clients that are different or even contrary to those your competitors are going to have.

Rule #7 Be Consistent

It is so important that you commit to your involvement in social media and networking, just like any other major role in your business. Budget for it. You will need to invest time, energy and money to get good at it. Initially, it is very important to pick what you are going to do in this time. It doesn't mean you have to be on Twitter, Facebook, LinkedIn, and video blogging all from the beginning. That would probably be overwhelming.

If you budget a half-hour a day, pick one social media platform you are comfortable with and start with that. If you are intimidated by video, we wouldn't suggest picking video right away, because it is probably going to be something that you quit pretty quickly.

You may need to experiment and test out a few mediums, but you will eventually need to commit to creating a consistent presence in a specific space. Choose something that you can develop some traction with and then expand from there. A blog is a natural place to start, but you need to connect it with the community using tools like Twitter, LinkedIn and Facebook. Each of these and others are discussed in greater detail in the next few chapters.

When someone gets excited and creates three blog entries, then leaves their website alone for a few months, it is the equivalent of trying to get well known in the business community by showing up for three networking events and not coming back for the next several months. It won't work. People want to know that you are committed, authentic, and they want to know you are going to be there. In business, it is difficult to find people you can depend upon. Once your online presence is created, a great thought leader will be there on a regular basis, becoming a pillar in the community.

If you're a human being, don't be afraid of being human. Don't be so professional that you become sterile and boring. Be professional, talk about business things, but also be yourself. When you are on networks like Facebook, it's OK to upload some family photos or holiday photos. We find that people comment more on our family photos or the last ski trip we went on than on our business video blogs. The key to developing trust is finding common ground and by letting people know who you are personally. It will help you establish more common ground. Common ground builds trust and trust drives the relationship.

"Most people work on a relationship to get a deal, but the reality is the relationship is the deal." - Bill Gibson, Chairman and Founder, Knowledge Brokers International

Chapter Five

Blogging

Your Home Base

With all of these social media and networking tools, it is crucial that we have a home base for all our media. We need an anchor for those who are connected with and following us. In order to be more than just part of the crowd, you need a central place for you to locate your branding, and your communications, where you can collect and connect with your network.

Blogs vs. Websites

A blog is an online diary where you write about your daily activities or thoughts. You can use your blog to keep the followers in your community up to date with whatever is going on in your business or your life. A website is more brochure-ware, showcasing your products and services, along with your contact information. Historically, a website is a little bit more static, with much less frequent updates.

Subscribing to blogs with RSS or other readers

Your audience can choose to subscribe to your blog, and never have to visit your website again, through the use of a feed reader. The dominant method for subscribing is through RSS, or Real Simple Syndication. Typically, when someone lands on your blog and decides they want to read it regularly, they click an RSS icon on your blog page to subscribe, and using feed readers, such as Google reader, Yahoo's reader, or other third party readers, they can now get regular updates from your blog. It's a way for you to connect and get subscribers, without them having to revisit your website each time you update it with a new blog entry.

A blog typically allows your readers the ability to get involved in the conversation. They can comment on your blog posts, either in response to the post itself or reacting to another reader's comment. Blog posts can actually grow and take on different directions as reader comments are posted. Good bloggers will engage in dialogue with their readers in the response section, addressing concerns or updating as new views are revealed.

Your blog can also serve as a jumping off point to other great resources. Something called track backs help with this. When another blogger writes about your blog entry and links to it, the blogging software will detect that and in the comments section let your readers know that someone else has referenced your blog on theirs. Most blogs that you will reference and link to will also do this for you. It's a great way to promote and be promoted by people and blogs that cater to a similar demographic. Blogging basically brings your website to life.

Should I Have a Website or a Blog?

There shouldn't be a question of having one or the other. You should have both, and ideally your blog is built in to your website. Your website would have your home page, your products and services, your videos, your contact information. Then you have the blog, where you can give personality to your business, your products and your services.

Who Should Blog? EVERYONE!

Who should blog? Everyone! Let's say you are a vice-president of sales for a manufacturer of bumpers for automobiles. You're in a niche business to business enterprise with perhaps only 10 customers, so why would you blog?

It enables you to access all levels of your corporate target market. While you might be dealing with just the buyer, beyond your one point of contact, several other people may be influencing whether or not the deal happens. Knowing you by name on a business card or one meeting in a board room, if anyone searches for you online, they are going to find your blog. They are going to hear your thoughts on the economy, see your pride in your products, and see you answering questions from consumers about the products and services you provide. This enables them to get to know you. They are shown more than one side of you, and actually can gain a greater understanding of your personal connection with the brand and who you are, so that when they meet you in person, they almost feel like they know you.

Viral Implications

Consider the following scenario: You write a blog that is of interest to senior executives. In time, you will find some of those executives starting to contact you. They may share the link to your blog with a few colleagues around the office, including someone at the C level or someone else you would consider a decision maker. If you consistently produce good quality content, people that matter to you will start to follow and read what you are doing. Before you know it, you will get that phone call seemingly out of nowhere. The person you would normally have to chase with emails and phone calls now contacts you. This is a reversal of the old sales model so that existing or potential clients are now calling you to talk more about your thoughts and opinions because like what you have to say.

Evil Corporate Bloggers

Only 16% of online consumers who read corporate blogs say they trust them.[9] One major reason for this lack of trust is that companies tend to approach a blog much like a press release or an advertising space. Few people truly believe what a company says in their advertising. However, if done properly, corporate blogs can work. Here are some common corporate blogging errors to avoid:

- ✓ When it is just another part of your collateral material, online brochure-ware. It's not a conversation, but is full of pitches and calls to action.
- ✓ It is just mostly a cutting and pasting of corporate announcements.
- ✓ There is no capacity for people to make comments.
- ✓ If it is possible for readers to make comments, these have to be approved by the blog owner before being posted. It appears that the blog owners are trying to censor what's being said on their blog rather than creating an open forum.
- ✓ The blog is not updated by an identifiable person. The blogger's name is posted as "administrator" versus "Sarah Reid, VP."

---

9   North American Technographics Media and Marketing Online Survey. Forrester Research Q2 2008 via the Groundswell Blog

All of these behaviors tell the reader, "This is not about you, and this is not about creating conversation or transparency." When people see this, they typically do not come back. Worse, they may even write negatively about it on their own wildly popular blog or Twitter profile.

Well, yes, but we don't call it "downsizing" any more. We call it our "Freedom to Blog" program.

Good Blogging Approach

A great blog should be structured like a great conversation. It should follow the same principles of use as other social media tools, which are about creating dialogue. Remember, it's not just about what we have to say it's also about listening to the customer, the participant. As thought leaders, we should be presenting our thoughts about our industry, the economy, the marketplace, even things we are passionate about personally, and allowing other people to get involved, get a dialogue going. Unfortunately most corporations see it as another extension of their PR, an over-controlled image. In a lot of cases, the consumer doesn't revisit that type of highly sanitized blog

Every Skyscraper Needs a Foundation

Blogging is a commitment. You can't start blogging and then quit in 90 days because it didn't work for you. Cultivating an interested community takes time and effort. Gary Vaynerchuk did 148 video blog entries before it started to really pay off. You need to spend time working, digging, and finding your voice. It's like building a skyscraper. You can drive by the big hole in the middle of the city and it looks likes nothing is happening. Then one day you look over and say "Wow, where did that building come from?" It takes effort and focus to build the foundation. Once created, however, it will start to pay, and for some it will pay big.

The longer you do it, the more content you build, and the bigger the reach your business will have. It's something that doesn't need to take a lot of effort, but it does take consistent effort.

"We Screwed up Royally"

On January 9th 2009, Hulu.com, a US based an online TV station, removed a number of on-demand episodes from their system without notifying their subscribers. An online revolt resulted. Subscribers freaked out about the fact that these shows were removed without any warning. A lot of companies with a traditional top down mentality would have just said too bad, the shows are free anyway. Jason Kilar, CEO of Hulu, used their blog and wrote an apology to the subscribers. Here's an excerpt:

> *"...this blog post is to communicate to our users that we screwed up royally with regards to how we handled this specific content removal and to apologize for our lack of strong execution. We gave effectively no notice to our users..."*

The entry goes into detail how they handled it poorly, and what they would do to resolve the situation. A lot companies would just point to the terms of use. Not Hulu.com. The lesson is to use your blog to deal with vocal customers, both happy and upset. Deal with them on a one-on-one basis, let your customers know that you are listening and you can and will make changes to grow your business. Once again we see the importance of transparency, and a blog is your home base for that.

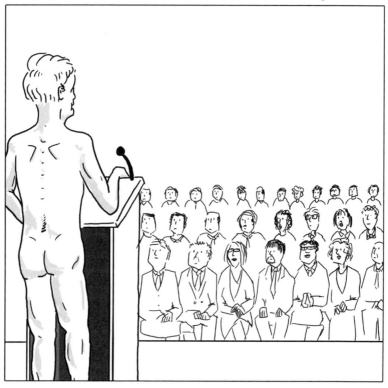

So - what do I mean when I talk about "radical transparency"?

Blogging Creates Continuity

"Trusted conversations have fragmented to the social web shifting the balance of power to communities. To regain trust, corporate websites will look more like a collection of real-time customer discussions not just product pitches." **Jeremiah Owyang** (Web-Strategist.com)

Use your social media and networking tools to expand and deepen your network, but anchor the relationship to your home base, your blog. You should be driving people to your website and your blog, and pulling content from your blog into those networks to share your insights and propagate your brand. Third party networks like Flickr, Twitter and Facebook tend to bury your content over time, drowning it out with noise. Your blog can give people easy access to your message and also pull in all the conversations about your brand into a more permanent and organized space.

People can search your blog on any topic you have talked about to see your thoughts, your corporate policies, and ask questions about any of your postings. Their questions and comments become part of your content and discussion base. They are there permanently. You do not want to use a third party social network as your anchor as you communicate, build a following, and create a brand, because you don't actually own your following on those social networks. They belong to the companies that provide that technology. They can terminate your membership, push ads from your competitors, and even go out of business. For a time, MySpace did extremely well, and then dipped off. What happens if Twitter runs out of money and shuts down? Overnight you'll lose the followers you have built up.

As those technologies rise and fall, which they will, you need to have a place on the internet that you own, where your community can gather and connect over the long term. Having your own domain and your own blog will help you establish a long term following and will add some continuity to your own online reputation and personality. Your blog is the ideal space for you to do this.

The Gutenberg Effect

The Gutenberg press, invented in 1436 in Germany, has been hailed as the catalyst for everything from the birth of the printing and news industry to a rise in nationalism and the resurgence of regional dialects in many parts of Europe. No longer needing dozens of people to hand scribe books, these presses could print hundreds of books in far less time than a team of scribes would take to produce one. Over time the barrier to entry for those wanting to share knowledge became drastically reduced. A boom in literacy followed in Europe and grew for hundreds of years afterward. No longer needing to wait for others to read to them or to translate Latin based texts to local dialect, many more people became well educated and empowered members of society. Many governments still rue the fact that they have to contend with literate, and therefore informed, citizenry. It makes them much more difficult to control.

When the concept of a weblog emerged over a decade ago, you either required programming skills to write and update your blog, or you needed to pay a programmer to do it. Creating RSS feeds was even more problematic. This was the modern day equivalent of hiring a team of scribes to publish your message. But this was just the beginning of the traditional text blog.

By 2001/2002 the term blogging began to creep into mainstream online communities and through traditional media. Tools like Blogger, TypePad, and more recently WordPress, came along that would enable people without a lot of technical background to blog. Their WYSWYG (what you see is what you get) editors and one click blog install software did for average people what the Gutenberg press did over 500 years ago. The blogosphere exploded. If you were tech savvy enough to use Microsoft Word you could operate these blogging tools. The barrier to entry had been lowered considerably. These simple blogging tools created a boom of bloggers that number in the tens of millions and is still growing.

Blogging with Different Types of Media

Text blogs is where it all started. We saw the beginnings of audio blogging, or podcasting in 2004/2005. A podcast comes in the format of an audio file, typically an MP3, which is compatible with most CD players, DVD players, and of course all forms of iPods and other portable digital players. Combined with a platform like WordPress, you can now syndicate your podcasts through systems like iTunes.

Once you become comfortable with your starting blog, you can consider expanding the repertoire of tools you use to create content. A mixed use of various forms of blogging can be particularly effective. Create some written blog entries, then link to or embed other people's videos, produce your our own videos, and once in a while upload an audio interview. Your listeners will respond to you in different ways. Some people like the audio, some like the video, while others will prefer text.

Google Loves Text

Let's talk about text. Google compiles its index by crawling web pages to search and catalog the text. Until Google and other major search engines can crawl audio and video, pulling out keywords using voice recognition, text is still crucial. Search engines still drive the majority of web traffic to blogs, and they work with text. Google and YouTube are beginning trials with voice recognition, but this won't likely have wide adoption for quite some time. It is worth noting that search engines tend to favor regularly updated blogs over static websites. Yet another reason to be consistent in your blogging.

Transcribe Your Audio and Video Posts

Until such time that the technology is available to search engines to automatically index audio and video, it is good practice to transcribe your audio and video files, or at least write a short outline with suitable key words. There are various relatively inexpensive outsourcing services that will do the transcriptions for you.

Content Management Systems

Content Management Systems (CMS) can help you integrate your blogs and podcasts with your website. Very little technical knowledge is required to operate a CMS.

The benefit of a CMS is that, once your website is built, you are able to log in just like you would a site like Facebook or MySpace, then in the back end you can update web pages, knowing very little about web technology or programming skills.

There are generic CMSs, open source CMSs, and also a very vertical specific or niche oriented tools that are developed for specific industries. A good example of an open source generic content management system is Mambo. Because of its open source nature, any one of thousands of developers globally can use it to build your website. Another major open source CMS tool is called Drupal. It's a fantastic tool that comes ready to install with most major hosting companies. WordPress is now more than just a blogging platform, and the right developer can set you up with a site that runs on WordPress but is also a fully functional CMS.

There are specific content management systems for automotive companies, financial advisors, and even for professional speakers and authors. Even if you're not in one of those vertical markets with a custom CMS it might be worthwhile using something like Ubertor or another CMS that has support built in to it. We have seen a lot of companies that will set up a WordPress, TypePad, or Blogger.com site that they quickly abandon because they can't get help on some of the most basic challenges. Sometimes paying a small fee for your product makes sense so that you have the support built in to it. Support can come in the form of coaching through bugs or website problems, or even video tutorials on how to perform specific functions on your site or blog. If you're going to go with WordPress or another open source tool budget monthly for potential paid support.

Being Held Ransom By Your IT Department?

Ideally, you are looking for a simple communications tool. Too many companies are shackled by their IT department, with response times slowed to a crawl waiting for the IT experts to update a page or approve the use of an application. Put easy to use tools in the hands of as many people as possible. Everyone should be an extension of sales and marketing.

Blogging Platforms

At present there are several blogging platforms that function well for most people. With Blogger, for example, you can get a sub-domain with your membership, such as mywebsite.blogger.com. Some platforms include built in podcasting plug-ins, and the sites tend to be very search engine friendly. They may include community elements, for collaboration with other bloggers.

While these blogging sites have some good tools, there are a few disadvantages to using them. Most end up looking identical to other blogger's sites. You are essentially building someone else's brand. Next week someone else could buy blogger.com, and decide to change the rules on you. Or its owner, Google, could decide it's not profitable and shut it down altogether. Some bloggers have been censored because blogger.com felt that what they were saying was not in line with their rules or code of conduct. So, if you want to be independent and develop a long-term presence as you grow your own brand, our suggestion is to use a stand-alone tool.

WordPress Self Hosted Blogs

Reserve a domain name and find a host. Don't start on WordPress.com or Blogger.com. There will be a lot of people to who disagree with us on this point, but if you are building your brand for your corporation, you need to go dig deep in your pocket and splurge on that $14 domain name, and the $5 hosting fee per month. It's not a lot of money. There are WordPress hosting companies that charge you $5 a month and can give you all the bells and whistles with nearly unlimited bandwidth.

Get your own domain name reserved through a system like GoDaddy.com, which is in our opinion the most ethical domain registrar in the market place. We have heard of other registrars not notifying website owners that their domain is about to expire, because they would rather just snap it up themselves or in a lot of cases they just are too disorganized to support you effectively.

When you are looking at hosting companies focus on either the bigger ones or a local one where you can have a relationship and access to the people that work at the company and can provide support. Companies like Amazon, with cloud computing and cloud hosting, are set up so you are not buying specific hosting packages or a specific server anymore. This trend towards cloud computing is going to create some significant changes.

Look closely at your hosting company. You want to make sure you are with a company that's big enough to handle these types of changes that are coming down. You don't want to have to move your site because they have gone down overnight and you got caught off guard. Make sure that they have the money to keep moving. That's why we are big fans of GoDaddy or Amazon.

Self-hosting enables you to customize the look and feel of your blog. There are tens of thousands of themes and plug-ins freely available to integrate into a user's blog. These enable you to begin building your own unique site and brand. If you go to Wordpress.org you can download their free open source software, which you then upload to your web server, and within a few minutes you can have a live blog. Most hosting companies now have an automatic install of WordPress blogging software.

WordPress is also better for search engine optimization than almost any other blogging platform. It's great for search engine optimization because it builds sites in the right structure and does most of the optimization automatically that other platforms require you to manually input, if they allow it at all.

If you find you need help to create your blog, you have a few options. If you live in a major city, you might attend a Word Camp. Once or twice a year, the local community of bloggers and programmers using WordPress get together and share best practices. It's a great way to meet others in the blogging community, and a good way to keep up to date on the latest ways to use these tools.

Alternatively, you can find a web professional to assist you in creating a simple or highly customized blog. Although you can launch a blog with very little technical knowledge, if you want customized functions or an original well branded look you will most likely need professional help.

If you are not a great techie, find one who is proficient in WordPress, probably through your local Craigslist. Or you could go to Meetup.com and look for your local blogging Meetup members. You will be able to find an expert on WordPress who can help you build your site. Typically a WordPress blog should cost you no more than $1000.00 dollars to get off the ground if you have someone else do it. If you want something highly customized and well branded expect to pay five to ten times that. You may be able to do it cheaper if you use an offshore developer through a site like elance.com.

What to Blog About?

There is a difference between a personal blogger and a business or professional blogger. A personal or life blog is generally a "Here's what I'm doing" affair. In business we want to be ourselves as we connect with people, but we also have to ask the important question, "What topic today or what theme for the next month is going to help the people who I am interested in doing business with?"

If I am targeting chief technology officers in corporations, then I am going to be blogging about things that interests them, not specifically about my product, possibly just issues in the industry, that having an unique slant to it. It could mean bringing in authorities or experts to interview for a video blog that is going to be of interest to the target audience.

Not talking too much about your products and services might seem counter-intuitive. What we're doing is providing unique content and solutions for our audience. We're elevating ourselves above the "pitch men" and are seen as trusted resources and peers of our target markets.

Just Get Started

The next step is to begin blogging, and don't be concerned about doing it perfectly to start. Even if you get going with just 150 words per day, writing them down and linking to something of interest, or doing a three-minute video blog entry, the key is to develop some consistency.

Don't worry if your blogs are not great at first. Part of blogging is finding your unique voice. The only people that they are going to be reading your blog when it first starts off will probably be your personal assistant, your mom, and your cousin. Once you have a number of entries and add content on a regular basis, search engines will begin to index you favorably based upon your subject matter. Once you start showing up in searches you will begin to see a trickle of traffic.

Create a plan, an outline for the long term content of your blog, so that you're not stuck for ideas on your second day attempting to write. As you proceed, sit down occasionally to brainstorm your next several blog topics in advance of needing to write them. Knowing what you'll write about ahead of time makes writing process so much easier. You do not want to be faced with a self-imposed deadline with no ideas at hand.

How John Chow makes $40,000 per month from Blogging

At the time of writing this book John Chow had surpassed $40,000 per month in earnings from his blog. We know John personally, and we follow him on Twitter and frequently bump into him at Meetups and Tweetups. John prides himself on working just a few hours a week and earning more than a full time income, all of it from revenues generated by blogging. John has written several great e-books that we have pored over and also have attended a number of his speaking events.

We sat down with John recently over a coffee and received a 70-minute download on blogging success.

John shared with us how he started. "JohnChow.com started off as a personal blog. I was an internet marketer before I was a blogger and I already understood how to turn visitors into dollars. When I realized the blog's potential I completely revamped it."

We have compiled this lengthy and valuable conversation into a series of tips on blogging and social media marketing that have helped him create success.

Tip #1 Your email list is your business

"Use your blog to convert visitors to your email list. Your email list is your business. If you add value, give them great content and great tools your list can become a banking ATM. This doesn't mean collecting e-mail addresses so you can blast them with offers everyday. My subscribers are double opt-in and broken down by interest group. Every email has to add value and appeal to the specific interests of the people subscribed. Every time you send out an email you can generate money. Too many people count visitors and RSS feed subscribers, but they don't seize the opportunity to more proactively market to them. Make sure you have a way to build a list from your blog. The best list building software I have seen is Aweber. I was banned from Google for 36 months and my list is what sustained me [the Google story is a whole other story]."

Tip #2 Have a sales funnel and process

"Once someone is on your list, have a series of free and paid products and programs that you market to them. I start off with several value added free programs such as my *How to Get Twitter Followers* program. Once they see results and use a few more of my other free tools and read my blog they often opt to buy into my premium programs."

Tip #3 Have your own product or something unique

"I had a good income from selling advertising on my blog, but I took some advice from John Reese that drastically increased it. I was selling advertising and other people's products off my blog, but John Reese suggested I also create and sell my own. People come to read what I have to say because I have built a relationship and trust. When I introduced my own products and programs my revenues jumped significantly and have continued to grow."

Tip #4 Write for your audience but always optimize for Google

"You don't want someone landing on your blog and see it stuffed with keywords. You should write about what your audience finds interesting. After you write your blog entry though, make sure you optimize it for search engines. Think about a title that your target market would search for. Your title has a big impact on whether or not you're found on Google. One of the ways that I write titles that get lots of traffic from Google is using the adwords keyword suggestion tool. [https://adwords.google.com/select/KeywordToolExternal]. I type in some keywords related to my entry and then Google tells me which are searched the most.

Tip #5 Use multiple media to promote your business

"When I have a promotion or new product launch I will use my blog, Twitter, and my email list to promote it. Twitter and email have a high instant response rate and represent two different groups of visitors. The blogging has less effect initially but unlike Twitter and email the blog entry will continue to get traffic for weeks or even years. Don't depend on any one tool, use them all together instead."

If You Build It They May Not Come

The next step is promoting your blog to stimulate some real momentum. Here are some strategies:

Offline:

Get your blog address on your business cards, brochures, and all other marketing materials. When you're out networking with people, talk to them about your blog.

Social Networking:

Post links to your blog on your LinkedIn, Face-Book, Twitter, and MySpace profiles and any other place you network socially. Most profiles have options to add additional information about your own sites, blogs and other social identities. Take advantage of this opportunity.

Social Bookmarking Sites:

Start using social bookmarking tools like Digg, Stumbleupon, and any of the other popular networks. You can usually add connections like you do in Twitter or Facebook and begin to vote for sites favored by your connections. In time they'll reciprocate. It's okay to Stumble or Digg your own site, just as long as you don't just bookmark yours exclusively.

With social bookmarking sites the whole idea is to share any and all great resources you find on the net. If you only share stuff you write or just promote your own site, it's no longer social. It's now 100% self-serving promotion and marketing, which is a turn-off for most people. The right Digg can deliver you dozens, hundreds and sometimes thousands of visitors. It's worth connecting with and adding value to the people on the networks.

Make it easy to find:

If your blog is separate from your website, display prominent links to the blog on your site. If your blog is connected to your site the same applies. Make sure there's a link promoting your blog in your email signature.

Connect with other bloggers:

Spend time on other blogs to build both links and community. Find the top bloggers in your region and in your industry and spend time on their sites. Read their blog entries, and make intelligent comments and additions to what they have to say. Most people are fine with your comments even if you disagree with them. They often leave space for you to put your blog address in the comments section. If your comment is relevant and interesting, you'll find that readers will tend to click through to see what else you have to say on your own blog.

Here are some examples of what a blog comment should **NOT** look like:

> *"Hi nice site. Check out mine http://Iamabigspammer. com"*
> *"I like what you write! We have great deals on new and used Jeeps!"*
> *"I agree! Read my entry on the subject at my blog"*

Or our personal favorite:

> *"HELLO VERY NICE BLOG ENTRY, YOU MAKE SOME SOLID POINTS AND I'M LOOKING FORWARD TO THE NEXT ONE!"*

These comments add no value and are an obvious attempt to siphon off visitors or just build links to their own site. Any good blogger will delete your comment and/or report it to various spammer databases that could eventually result in all of your comments on any WordPress driven blog to be seen as spam automatically. Blogging is about community. Get good at building community and you will have all the traffic and the links you need.

Blogging levels the playing field. You can get just as much traffic, if not more, than a competitor 10 times your size if you create good content and a loyal following. If you understand the concept of social media interaction, develop great content and are consistent, you can build a much larger following. You have at your fingertips the modern version of the Gutenberg Press. What you do with that opportunity is up to you.

Chapter Six

Online Video

Why online video is great

When you meet somebody in person you have a whole bunch of tools in your sales arsenal. You have your smile, your handshake, your outfit, your smell and your words. All these things affect the impression people have of you.

The internet takes away many of these rapport-building tools and can impersonalize things. Video is the closest thing you have to an in-person meeting, because it equips you with many rapport-building tools. People can see your smile, hear your enthusiasm, see what you are wearing, and experience your passion about a certain topic.

It is so valuable in your business to put out good quality video. By quality we mean quality content, not quality production. Forget investing thousands of dollars in video equipment. When you start, just get it out there for people to watch. But make sure it's made of substance that they will want to watch.

Video blogging is different from written blogs because video makes it very difficult for you to be misquoted. When people are sharing your information they will have to embed your entire video, not just the section they are quoting.

The power of online video is not high production values. Sure, that is important for advertisements of big brands like Coca-Cola or someone producing the next

season of a hit TV program, but for individual sales professionals and marketers this is not required. Online
video is about a very personal conversation that builds a
following. Don't worry if your videos are not broadcast
quality. That's what HDTV is for.

Is Video Blogging Hard?

The best thing about video blogging is that it's quick
and it is easy to do. Most likely you already own a device that allows you to capture video, whether it be a cell
phone, web cam, or digital camera. Beyond that, the most
important criteria is that it is easy to use. You will have to
learn how to upload and edit your videos, but there are a
number of software choices available to make this process
relatively simple. The more compact and mobile your
video enabled device the higher the chance you will video
blog regularly. Some people get hung up on video quality
but a portion of the most viral videos and most popular
video bloggers appear very amateur looking. The reason?
People want content and authenticity. If they wanted polished they'd watch an MTV reality TV show.

How to Get Started

Begin by creating a basic script, so you can produce
a concise video segment that grabs and holds attention
without rambling. Next, upload your clip to YouTube,
Viddler, Vimeo or similar websites to which you can direct
links and traffic.

How to Get Distribution

Video allows for wide distribution. There are dozens
of major video distribution sites and hundreds of niche
sites. The major video posting and distribution sites you
can add video include:

✓ Viddler (Viddler.com)
✓ YouTube (YouTube.com)
✓ Yahoo Video (video.yahoo.com)
✓ Vimeo (Vimeo.com)
✓ Blip.tv (Blip.tv)
✓ HowCast (Howcast.com)
✓ Graspr (graspr.com)

For most people, using YouTube, Viddler or Blip.tv will suffice. There are tools available that allow you to upload to all of these networks at once. One tool that allows you to potentially get your videos out to thousands of people is tubemogul.com. This website allows you to syndicate your video to multiple platforms at the same time, so don't have to sit there and upload to YouTube, Vimeo, Blip.tv, and Viddler separately.

Don't overlook iTunes

Another audience, which is by no means slowing its growth, is the iTunes audience. If you are going to be video blogging, one suggestion is to utilize WordPress and an iTunes plug-in like Power Press. On top of uploading to Tubemogul, you should also upload to your own web site and link to the files from your blog. Once you have your blog setup with "Power Press" or another podcasting plug-in, you can register your blog feed in iTunes. Once approved, anyone with an iPod, iPhone or iTunes on their computer can automatically get your videos delivered to them via iTunes every time you add a new video.

Create a Hook

Your format should help you create a bit of a distinction or a signature. Try to find a way to create a memorable opening that is consistent throughout your videos. The next step is to deliver your content in a manner that is engaging, using contrast, special guests and bold or unique perspectives. Contrast is about varying the content and format throughout the video clip. In doing this we keep people's interest.

Your video's finish should include a call to action or a memorable and brief statement that includes your domain name, email or some other way that they can contact you. This is important because if your videos are widely distributed they may be on sites, blogs or shared in networks that don't have links to your site or mention of how to contact you.

How many video bloggers are going to be around in 6 months? Gary Vaynerchuk's stand on this is that there is room for a Gary Vaynerchuk of every industry and there are not many yet. He says even the wine industry has room for another Gary Vaynerchuk. There could be someone doing a show on wines from the Napa Valley, or a Blend Wine Show that discusses only blends. An example in another industry would be Ian Watt, where Ian is focused on blogging on condos and townhouses in the downtown Vancouver real estate market. There is room for many more real estate video bloggers in the Vancouver area, even in the downtown core – just do it differently than Ian and focus on a different niche.

When it comes to video, there are two questions that regularly arise. First, what should I talk about? And second, how long should it be? The easiest way to select topics is to look in your email inbox and review the questions that you are asked by potential customers. Create answers to questions that you may think are basic, but sometimes you forget that lots of people don't know. As for the length we like to produce video with a two minute maximum. Just pound out little pieces of information answering a specific question or a specific topic. Holding an audience for much longer is unlikely, so get your licks in while you can.

Try to do this every day of the week, creating consistency. Initially, this will be a big challenge for some of you, but it gets easier as you make it part of your habit. Start of with a short format that is easy to commit to. You can always have longer segments on special topics, or if you choose to occasionally interview a guest

If you begin to run out of content, why not invite other thought leaders on your show to share their opinions. This achieves two things. It gives your followers interesting new content, but it can also attract a different audience that may be following your guest.

Interviewing Experts is a Great Way to Position Yourself

Note From Stephen Jagger: In 2007 I went to the Pubcon Conference in Las Vegas, NV with Rodney Bartlett (from Reachd.com) to learn, mingle and shoot some video with some of the brightest minds in the search engine world. We brought down our video camera with the plan to conduct some interviews with some key individuals. Not only did we get interviews with Craigslist.org's Craig Newmark and Demand Media's Richard Rosenblatt but also we got the chance to speak with Google's Matt Cutts.

Matt is the Head of Web SPAM at Google and is partially responsible for what you see when you search for something within Google. Having the opportunity to speak with Matt and ask him questions that web designers, developers, business owners and search engine optimizers would love to know the answers to helped position Reachd.com as an "in the know" and "connected" organization. What we did not know is how many people would want to watch this interview. At the time of publishing this book, over 30,000 people have watched this interview and it has helped us get students into our workshops, consulting deals and speaking opportunities.

Another novel idea was tried out by Kye Grace, a Vancouver realtor, who ran a 72-hour open house promotion where he stayed out for three full days, video streaming it to 1300 unique viewers. Even more people viewed the property online and interacted with him than actually walked through the open house.

By integrating these tools into your existing sales and business processes, you can greatly expand your potential audience, far beyond the few that might wander by your tradeshow booth or through your open house or other event.

Probably one of the best ways to start off is to get a video on your home page. Create a 30 second video explaining who you are and what you do.

Customer created testimonial videos expressing their thoughts and feelings on your products or services can be very valuable as well.

Sometimes Value Added Can Mean Fun Added

Fun videos, like the ones you find on WillItBlend.com, are a fantastic format for engagement. They manufacture commercial and home use food and beverage blenders that will blend just about any thing. They have dropped everything into the blender from a BlackBerry and an iPhone to skis, toy cars and even rocks. If it was a boring product testing video they could expect no audience, but because they find outrageous things to throw in a blender it creates faith in the product quality, while entertaining and engaging their audience.

BuildDirect.com used indoor laminate flooring to cover the outdoor deck of their 19th floor penthouse office. Each week they would torture and abuse the floor and then post the video of it for people to see. They built a special site for the project called WatchUsWreckAFloor.com. This was carried out in the middle of the winter, the rainy season in Vancouver. It also snowed, a much less common occurrence in the city. They had special theme days for floor wrecking: Bring your dog to work day (yes they did do their business on the floor), hockey day, complete with nets, sticks and real Canadian hockey fights, live chickens in the office day, and lastly a high heels night that ended with a contest involving a pick-axe. After almost a month the only thing it didn't stand up to was the pickaxe. This got them noticed by bloggers, other people in their industry and resulted in several sales to new clients as well.

Creating one video that is intended to go viral doesn't usually work. Consistently video blogging, trying new things over time usually is what it takes to go viral. Remember Gary Vaynerchuk, who took 148 video blogs before he found the right formula. Be patient, be creative, and be consistent.

Chapter Seven

Micro-blogging

Micro-blogging refers to a type of online content publishing that enables users to produce short updates. It includes tools such as Twitter, Friendfeed, Yammer, and a number of other applications that allow you to do brief updates. This can include rather short text messages, typically up to 140 characters, and brief audio or video broadcasts. There are a number of platforms available to users. Most social networks have some sort of micro-blogging or "status update" options built into their websites for their users to update each other on what they are doing or thinking.

What Are You Doing? What Are You Thinking?

The idea behind micro-blogging platforms is to put your message in a simple condensed form. Twitter, for example, allows 140 characters to answer the question, "What are you doing?" With micro-blogging you don't have the opportunity to write big, long blog posts. Micro-blogging means you are limited in how much you can type. Many updates on Twitter are actually more focused on what people are thinking or feeling than what they are actually doing.

Micro-blogging platforms provide a quick and easy way for you to keep your community and connections up to date with what you are doing. It's a very simple business tool, with a very simple business model that has exploded.

The great thing about it and the reason it works for business is that it allows you to create conversations with like minded individuals, talk to potential customers and contacts about who you are, what you do, and interact with people. These conversations potentially lead to new business by opening the communications channel in a casual ultra-permission-based way.

Why we describe it as ultra-permission-based is that at any moment with a click of one button people can un-follow your updates. This puts a lot of pressure on the marketer or communicator to stay relevant and non-pitchy.

It's also a way to also establish yourself as a thought leader by adding value to the people following your updates. The biggest challenge to traditional direct mail marketers in moving forward with tools like Twitter is they misunderstand their utility.

Twitter

Twitter is a free micro-blogging platform that allows you to broadcast your daily business (and even personal) thoughts and activities to a group of followers or subscribers. This may seem like a "fringe" or obscure activity, but mainstream media, politicians, business leaders and entrepreneurs now use the tool

Friendfeed

Friendfeed is another micro-blogging platform that at first glance looks a lot like Twitter. It is used more as an aggregator or single stream of all of your social media activities. When you register you can enter the information from all of your social media platforms such as Facebook, Twitter, YouTube, and your blogs.

Whenever you update any of these it is automatically posted to your "feed." Unlike Twitter your comments and posts can be lengthy and include multimedia such as video and photographs. You can also set it up so that what ever you enter directly into your Friendfeed status updates is also shared with your Twitter connections.

Twitter's Power Comes from Being Bi-Directional

We recently overheard a marketer refer to Twitter as a "billboard" where you can post limited time specials and news blasts for free. We cringed. This is not what a networking event or social gathering is about, and Twitter is closer to a networking function in its applications than it is to a billboard or even a blog.

Twitter is a bi-directional communications tool. A lot of traditional media and marketers that get on the tool initially only see it as one-way. Those who embrace it as a two-way communications tool are the ones that are building real relationships and connections.

You don't have a choice in who follows you, they choose to follow you. It's not like the people who drive by a billboard or have to watch an ad on TV. You can't make anybody follow you, and they can un-follow you in an instant. Be of value, or at least be entertaining and non advertorial.

It's an interesting way of thinking about your communication, where you actually have to be helpful to others, help other business owners, and create the conversation with them to learn more about who they are and what they do. Business will come out of that. It's a process of deepening engagement levels. You will start meeting people you would never have met and you will start doing business with people that you would have never had the opportunity to do business with otherwise.

People seem to have a lower and lower threshold for noise, or at least with all of the noise coming from all types of media it is more difficult to be heard. If you go to Google's news front page, you will notice very succinct headlines with a few words of text, allowing you to scan them and see which articles interest you. Twitter is a collection of real time headlines on people's lives. It encourages entrepreneurs, writers, bloggers, or community activists to write concisely, adding value in shorter periods of time. People today want bite size pieces of information when they want it. Twitter fills that demand.

It's Not the Number of Followers It's The Number of Relationships

It's not about counting the number of people who are following you on Twitter or tools like Friendfeed. It is wiser to count how many relationships have you developed. "How have you added value today?" is the question we need to ask, not "How can I get visitors to my product page now?"

Someone on Twitter who has read your postings and clicked through to your website is a qualified person. They have already been introduced to you and some of your ideas, and therefore have some expectation of what they are going to read. It's not a random click from a search engine, which has bounce rates up over 85% in a lot of cases (Bounce rates are the percentage of people that immediately leave a website after loading a page).

We are hesitant to write "Rules" for using Twitter. It has multiple applications depending on your own network, career path, social behavior and goals. With that said, if you're using it for business and sales we have put together a few guidelines to think about when using Twitter.

Twitter is for Listening not just Broadcasting

Twitter is a combination of blogging and communications and it's rather rapid. A good quote from Warren

Whitlock, co-author of the Twitter handbook (quote sent to Shane via Twitter), was "Traditional marketing, if they stop listening, just be louder. Social media marketing, listen to the customer and serve them."

In addition to creating messages and broadcasting them, we are also listening to our customers and peers. There is a function within Twitter that can be found at search.twitter.com, allowing you to search keywords about your business or your industry or products or services. You can see, by the minute, what the five million people on Twitter had to say about you or your wares in the last day, week, month, or within a specific time frame. If you go into the "advanced" search option you can narrow your search to a specific geographic region and time frame.

Nick Usborne author of the book *Networds* was not initially a Twitter fan. When first invited to Twitter he saw it as a time waster, but over a period of time has come to see it as a valuable tool. When we interviewed him via Skype he had an interesting outlook on Twitter and the internet. Here were some of the highlights from the discussion:

#1 The internet is fragmenting and readers have less time for more media

"Readers now have very fragmented attention. Newspapers are disappearing because their relationship with the reader ceased to have depth. What's happening is that people don't have time to read much more than 140 characters. The click through trends on my email newsletters tell me this. It's evident that people only scan sections or headlines before clicking through to what they want."

#2 It has always been about connecting people to people.

"I wrote Networks in 2001, and not much has changed. In fact not much has changed in a decade. Before it was a graphic interface, it was about people who share common interests connecting. It has always been about people talking to people. Alt.sex, alt.drugs, alt.rockandroll were the first three news groups online, enabling people to connect with other people and find information. These are still dominant topics. Twitter's success is connected to this, it's a way for people to connect with people at 140 characters at a time. Marketers have always struggled with the true utility of the web. It's bi-directional, not a broadcast medium, and it's about people."

#3 Twitter is a great marketing medium

"If used to talk with and listen to your customers, Twitter is a great marketing tool. My newsletter has always been a very important part of my business over the past 10 years. Today Twitter is proving to be very important as well. In many cases I am getting a higher click through rate on my 140 character Tweets than I am on some of my newsletter headlines. Part of it is that the people on Twitter have chosen to follow my updates and connect with me."

Get All Levels of Your Organization Engaged

One organization we mentioned earlier that uses social networking very well is Zappos. Zappos uses Twitter in a very interesting way as they monitor the conversation about their business online and then engage their customers or critics in real time while the conversation is fresh. They encourage all their staff to be on Twitter, and most are. The Zappos website has links to everybody's Twitter profile and updates all the way from the CEO to brand new frontline staff. It's a great start toward running a transparent business, having all your people on the internet and using Twitter to engage with existing and potential customers.

The $24 Billion Tweeting CEO

Interview with Peter Aceto, CEO of ING Direct Canada

ING Direct is an online bank with 1.6 million customers and $24 billion in assets under management. Its core mandate is to provide a fair, transparent, no strings attached banking experience for the average consumer. In short, ING is revolutionary and disruptive in nature, both in their use of technology and in customer engagement strategies.

We found Peter Aceto, @CEO_INGDirect, through a Twitter connection in Toronto, and within just a few weeks we began to develop a good rapport. It started off with Shane and Peter's common interest in leadership and their respective leadership tweets. About a week before heading to Toronto to speak at the Massive Tech Conference we sent Peter a short Twitter direct message asking him if we could take him for dinner and interview him for *Sociable!* After a couple e-mails back and forth we agreed on a time and a place. This already was impressive that a CEO not only talked about engagement on Twitter but also walked his talk, and was open to direct dialogue and meeting in person.

Peter got on Twitter based upon the advice of Bruce Philp, founder of GWP Brand Engineering and co-author of "The Orange Code." Bruce, known as @BrandCowboy on Twitter, suggested that Twitter was a place where ING should be. In Peter's own words, he wants to be "where my customers are." This was already evident from Peter's leadership style. You will often find him in the call center taking customer calls, talking with staff and seeing what is happening on the frontlines. It's evident that he sees his organization's success as closely tied to direct employee and customer engagement.

When we asked Peter about his strategy in launching his Twitter presence he said, "I took Bruce's advice to not be afraid and just do it." For ING Direct Twitter fit into an ongoing strategy for transparency and engagement with customers and employees.

"It is risky for most of my competitors to come into social media. Their strategy is not one of transparency. Banking is not transparent. ING direct wants to be open and transparent."

When we asked Peter what he Tweets about he said, "It's mostly personal, I want it to be a close representation of who I am, what I am doing to engage my staff and customers." Peter doesn't update a lot about marketing or ING promotions.

Peter's ING corporate Twitter presence has garnered him multiple media interviews and conference speaking opportunities. All of this from just a few tweets a day.

Conversations Lead to Customers You Don't Know

Note from Stephen Jagger: While writing this chapter of the book, I posted an update in Twitter about a real estate agent that had called me asking about a 72 hour open house. I received three responses within three minutes, one of them a real estate agent in Minneapolis. He asked me the question, "How did the 72 hour open house turn out?" Now I have engaged a real estate agent from Minneapolis, who is an ideal candidate for my product Ubertor. We had a great conversation, but we were not talking about my product, we were talking about my business and his business and getting to know each other. The great thing is there were no cold calls, mass emails or brochure mailings involved, just a brief conversation that unearthed a qualified prospect.

Having conversations online with a tool like Twitter takes the fear out of saying yes to doing business. If someone has been following our Twitter updates, they know what seminars we have attended, they see the questions we ask, they watch how we contribute to the community, and they follow the links to our blogs. It's a constant update, a stream of consciousness coming from us online as to what we are doing, what we are about, and how we are adding value. They also get to see who endorses us by observing who is following us and who is communicating with us. By the time someone meets us they already feel that we have a certain level of relationship we would not have otherwise.

Twitter Thaws the Cold Call or Cold Event

Engaging in online dialogue with strangers eases the tension in first "real world" meetings, because the parties are no longer strangers. As an example, we recently attended a business function, and each of us had someone walk up and say, "Hey, I am Fred from XYZ company and I have been following you on Twitter and I appreciate what you had to say about [fill in the Twitter comment or blog topic]," so when we met them offline, they already felt like they knew us. We also felt a lack of tension in the air, because even though most people there had never met each other in "real life," we all had relationships on Twitter.

It's a fantastic tool to create transparency, for better or for worse, by being a bit human, possibly writing, "Hey, I just locked my keys in my house." That seems like a ridiculous thing to announce to the universe, but when you get twelve empathetic messages back, plus a few people digging you with a little bit of humor, it makes us seem human and approachable.

> **Note from Shane Gibson:** I had a new acquaintance that I met through Twitter tell me that she had seen me several times at business functions but didn't know how to approach me. She told me following me on Twitter made me more approachable and eventually lead to her saying hello and making the business connection. I didn't realize that I seemed unapproachable at events, but by creating a new channel for people to get to know me more personally I have reaped great benefits. Twitter has really helped me take the chill out of networking.

Make Time for Leveraged Marketing Efforts

Twitter is asking for a 140 character answer to a very simple question, "What are you doing?" Of course, the comment from many people is, "That takes a lot of time." But how long does it take to write 140 characters? If you wrote eight tweets per day, it should take you less than 15 minutes. If you do that, you would be above 60% to 70% of the people on Twitter. In other words, you would be more engaged than most. To be ahead of the curve, you just need to be consistent and write regular updates on what you are doing or thinking.

If you can't afford those 15 minutes a day because you are too busy, something is probably wrong with your marketing activities. Is there anything you're still doing that is no longer giving a good return on investment for your time? Review these things you are doing that are making you feel too busy. You may decide to cut a flier you're distributing to a certain target group, or you could be cutting out the time you spend reading news sites or other activities that aren't giving you a high ROI.

If you're a do-it-yourself marketer for your business and you spend several hours a week on your website's search engine optimization, maybe it's time to outsource and spend your time getting social instead. What's your time worth? What are you doing to leverage it? Once you start seeing the success of Twitter or the other social media and networking tools, ideally you will start cutting other things out of your work life because Twitter or tools like it actually make you more efficient and more effective.

Note From Stephen Jagger: During a presentation to a group of real estate professionals, one agent said he did not have time to be involved in something like Twitter. So I opened up my Twitter account and posted a message. My Twitter and Facebook are integrated, so I was able to update several thousand people on what I was up to in less than 15 seconds. Then I asked, "How long did that take as a opposed to writing a lengthy email that is sent out to 2000 people but gets caught up in spam filters or junk folders?" He didn't have an answer. His whole office is on Twitter now.

When someone responds to you on Twitter, a lot of other people see that and it begins to propagate. This expands your audience base, as followers of the respondent, who may not have been following you, are now exposed to the conversation. It creates a viral or geometric increase in the number of people who see what you do.

Master the Art of Conversational Connecting

People won't listen to you if it's all about you or it's all chatter or all business. Spend some time replying to other people's conversations and getting involved.

Note from Shane Gibson: Each morning I put one or two inspirational quotes on my Twitter stream. When I update my blog in the afternoon, I will put a link to it on Twitter usually in the form of a question, such as, "What's your leadership profile?" Throughout the day and evening I will respond and connect with other people and even retweet (which means forward another person's message over to my network). This promotes other people, and helps them get responses. My goal is to have a good balance of 70% conversation with the community, and 30% about what I am doing or what my business is about. This helps me come off not as a pitch artist or a taker, but instead as a positive contributor to the community.

We need to ask our self the questions: "How can I add value? How can I get involved in the conversation? How can I make it about them?" The more we can contribute to our network of followers, the quicker it's going to grow and the larger our influence is going to become. If we're helping and building other people up it creates numbers but more importantly it creates strong loyal participants. Anyone who tells you that Twitter is a get rich quick tool is seriously misguided. Just like all other forms of human interaction, it takes time to build credibility and a sustainable revenue stream.

22 Types of Updates You Can Post on Twitter

1. Where you are physically located a given moment
2. A link to a picture of an event you are attending
3. A question about a business challenge
4. A question about a popular topic in the news
5. Share a link to your most recent blog entry
6. Share a tip on your area of expertise
7. Share a link to a breaking news story
8. Retweet someone else's update that your followers would find useful
9. Answer someone else's question
10. A link to a picture of a social outing
11. A link to a diagram that would explain a business process or idea
12. A link to an event you are promoting or that is happening in the community
13. A link to a community event of value
14. A link to a sale or business promotion that will save people money

15. Promote a person who just joined Twitter
16. Promote and thank some of your favorite people on Twitter
17. Thank someone who has linked to your blog or retweeted your updates
18. Upload a photo of a sunset or your natural surroundings
19. Praise someone for great content they have created
20. Review a restaurant, movie or business in 140 characters or less.
21. Share some of you favorite quotes
22. Share a link to a white paper or press release

These are just some of the types of updates you can post on tools like Twitter or Friendfeed. The key to having an engaging Twitter feed is contrast. Contrast in conversations you have with people offline is also what keeps things interesting. On Twitter this holds true as well. By varying the types of tweets you post it will keep people more engaged than if you were to only to post one type of tweet.

Anyone of these types of posts done too repetitively will cause people to tune you out or simply unfollow you. It would be like hanging out with someone who only talked about one subject or who only asked questions. It would be unnatural, not to mention awkward. By varying what you write about in your updates and keeping it conversational, you can make sure that those following you stay engaged through bi-directional communications and content that has contrast or variation.

Are You Followable?

People are unlikely to follow your Twitter stream unless your profile provides background information on who you are. Include a link to your personal website. If you don't have a website, at least link to your LinkedIn profile, your corporate website, even your Facebook or MySpace profile. This way, potential followers can see you as a real human being, rather than a computer generated marketing node or some sort of digital lurker.

Invest the time to upload a photo of yourself and write a nice bio. Make that bio less pitchy, and more straight forward. You will find that people feel less threatened and more open to following you if you do this. Your Twitter profile is a landing page. It shouldn't be about your pitch, but rather about becoming trusted and referable. When your profile is properly built, you will find it's easier to attract followers and to pass on your messages to others.

Take time to customize the background of your Twitter page. When you are logged into Twitter there is a settings option you can click. You will then see a "design" tab where you can select the option of "change background image." We would strongly suggest that you have someone design an image for you that is consistent with your personal or corporate branding. It will allow people to learn more about you than the 160-character bio that Twitter allows you to add to your profile.

Note From Stephen Jagger: Definitely have your photo on your profile. The other day I was at a cocktail party with my wife, just about to get nametags, when a woman walked by and said, "Hi Steve Jagger. You don't know me, but I follow you on Twitter." We talked for a few moments, and then she went on her way. My wife exclaimed, "Wow, how does that happen? Because she is reading your updates?" I said, "Yes, she is reading the updates, but she also sees my picture 12 times a day, it makes it easier to associate a name with a face that way."

It's personal reputation and brand building and it makes us approachable. Traditionally, we would make ourselves distant because we are business experts, in the past being untouchable and aloof helped a professional's brand. Today, people want the real deal, not a constructed and polished image.

If someone walks through your door selling a hi-tech solution, and you have never met them, there are a lot of questions about their credibility. A big part of the sales process is not about the solution but spending time gaining trust.

If you were following this same person on Twitter for some time and have seen 200 updates from them, there is a lot more trust already because this is not your first encounter. Frequency of contact plus genuine value-added interactions builds trust and relationships.

The Big Question: How Do I Get Followers?

There are many ways to get followers on Twitter. A better question to ask is, "How do I get the right followers on Twitter?" There are online software programs that will follow everyone on Twitter that talks about a certain key term such as "car insurance." Many of these people will follow you back. In fact, a lot of people who only focus on how many followers they get will have it set so they auto-follow everyone who follows them.

Unless you're selling car insurance or widgets to everyone on the planet then this method probably is unadvisable. You don't want to follow everyone's updates, only people who are in your target market or those that have engaging conversations or content to share.

Most of the auto-follow crowd is not into conversations, they just tend to publish links, playing a numbers game as they look for more followers. You want people that are listening to you, and in turn you want to be listening to the right people. Manually selecting people to follow one-by-one, although time consuming will help you create quality relationships and build a desirable community.

Hi! We've never met, but I noticed you stopped following me on Twitter a few hours ago. Mind if I ask why?

You only need one quality contact to change your life or take your business to the next level. In fact, if you only have 100 followers but you have had great conversations with all of them and are doing business with five of them you have achieved a greater success than many people who have 2000 followers but have not engaged people.

16 key strategies that we used to grow our Twitter following "organically"[10]

1. Produce great content on multiple channels and platforms

If you produce great content on your blog, YouTube channel, and are great at connecting with people on other social networks then people will seek you out on Twitter. They will want to know what you're doing and when you're posting your next great video, podcast or blog entry. Focusing on unique and engaging content, and dialogue on multiple platforms will increase your community size on all of them including Twitter.

2. Twitterize your social media destinations

Make sure you have a "follow me on Twitter" icon prominently displayed on every page of your blog and website. It doesn't have to be a huge button but it should be prominent. Within Facebook, LinkedIn, YouTube and any other social media destination make sure you have obvious links back to your Twitter profile. Once people experience your great content or have engaging dialogue with you, you want to make it easy and obvious for them to follow you on Twitter.

3. Promote your twitter profile offline

---

10   Organic growth refers to building a following by being engaging and authentic and not participating in Twitter ponzi schemes, auto follow robots etc.

Have your Twitter ID on all your collateral materials. This includes any books, magazines or newsletters you publish. In addition, have your Twitter profile on your business cards, name tag at events, tradeshow booth, and anything else that the public sees.

4. Have a good follower to following ratio

People tend to follow people on Twitter that they know are listening. They want to know that you care about what they have to say. If you're following 200 people and have 4000 followers the message you are sending is, "I'm not listening, I'm just broadcasting." Unless you're a rock star or a celebrity, people will be unlikely to follow you if they think there's a minimal chance that you will follow them back.

The converse is also true. If you're following 1000 people and only have 100 followers people will assume that you're not listening, you're just following them to get followed back. The key is to take your time, apply all 16 strategies and over a period of months (not weeks) and you will assemble a substantial following.

5. Search for people and conversations that resonate with you

Using search.twitter.com you can search for key words that your potential prospects or partners would be talking about. Ubertor searches for and connects with people that talk about real estate and technology. Doolin's Irish pub (@doolins) searches for people nearby their location who talk about beer, or watching sports matches on

TV. Once you find those people, sort through the robots and broadcasters, and just follow the ones who are engaging in genuine dialogue and sharing great ideas or insights. If your profile and bio resonate with their interests they will often follow you back.

6. Build a strong local network

Most of us, regardless of the global reach of our business opportunities, should establish a strong local network. Follow and connect with other people in your city. Promote what they're doing and see what you can do to help them out. You will have a higher chance of developing strong ties with local business people because there will be opportunities to connect in person, and you already have something in common. Although your network will extend globally, you will find that your strong local contacts will promote you and your business if you have established a rapport with them.

7. Follow retweeters

Often several people will pass on your good tweet. People you don't know will do many of the resulting retweets. You might want to investigate if you should follow those people, as they have already proven they like what you have to say and there's a good chance they will follow you because of this.

8. Follow people who follow your competitors

If your competitors have a strong online engagement strategy then there's a good chance that they have a good concentration of quality connections on Twitter. If their interest revolves around a service you provide or blog content that you create then there's a good chance they will follow you back. Be wary of following people who are connected to competitors if your competitors are not engaging or have a weak Twitter strategy, as there's a good chance their follower quality and relevancy for you will be low.

9. Follow people who talk about your competitors

Whether they talk positively or negatively about your competitors, they have an interest and may even be spending money in your business or industry. Engage these people and you will begin to develop a rapport with them.

10. Use Twellow.com to target key people and groups

Twellow is a comprehensive Twitter directory. It includes millions of Twitter profiles organized by geography, industry and various industry sub-categories. If you want to target CEOs working for IT companies in Texas, it will provide you a list of people to follow. Highly organized and easy to register and use, we consider this a key tool for anyone serious about building a targeted Twitter following.

11. Contextualize your tweets when following to be followed

Often when you're networking the first few minutes of a conversation will help you determine if you will stick around and socialize. The same thing goes for Twitter. Think about the people you are trying to attract and make sure your Twitter updates will reflect their interests, stature and culture. This will increase the chance of them following you.

For example, if you used Twellow to find CEOs then you most likely would write Twitter updates that interest them. You would follow 40 or 50 CEOs, many of whom would check out your profile to see what you are about. You could quote Warren Buffet, then link to an article on leadership and maybe retweet a couple well-known CEOs as well. You want to have a conversation that CEOs would follow. The idea is to make sure that your dialogue matches the market you are targeting.

12. Watch your tweet frequency

You could lose out either way. If you don't create sufficient updates you won't show up in a lot of searches, and people will often miss your sporadic updates.

If you update too much, you risk being called "noisy" and filling up people's Twitter stream. This may get you unfollowed. However, we have found that being a bit too noisy pays off more than being too quiet. A safe volume of updates in a day is 10 to 15. Spaced out well, this will give you a higher chance of being noticed and creating a dialogue. If you are working in several time zones you may want to pre-schedule some tweets using a tool like hootsuite.com to post tips or links to valuable information while you're sleeping as well. The key is to update regularly, but make sure your tweets are of value and that you use a diversity of tweets.

If you're not updating regularly your chances of getting new followers greatly decreases.

13. Hold Tweetups

A Tweetup is an offline meeting of Twitter people. Anyone can announce one, but the organizer usually is responsible for arranging the venue. We helped organize Tweetups with over 100 people in attendance with less than 48 hours notice. It quickly allows you to make personal connections with the people you have been chatting to online and establish deeper rapport. If your following is large enough or if you're connected to the right people you can even plan Tweetups in cities you are visiting.

14. Pay it forward

Through the seminars that we do on stages across four continents, we have been able to teach and motivate people to use social media tools. We also sit down one on one with friends and associates to give tips and pointers on how to get started. People in both groups end up being some of our best online promoters, and we return the favor. Take time to teach one person each week how to use Twitter effectively. At the end of one year you will have 52 teammates all cheering for each other.

15. Cooperate with competitors

Form alliances and joint Tweet campaigns with people that have the same target market as you. You can each double your following over a short period of time. This may seem risky at first, but if you both have quality connections one has to realize that there are many more to be made, and by promoting each other you double your reach quickly and leapfrog along the typical exponential growth curve in followers.

16. Get involved in the conversation

Don't just lurk, chat! When you see someone make a good point or even just a casual comment that you like, respond. If it's on topic and timely often a person that is not following you will appreciate the dialogue and take an interest in you. The more you chat and are community focused the more trust and exposure you can garner.

Interview with Ryan Holmes CEO of Invoke Media

Invoke media is the creator of the Twitter application Hootsuite. We asked Ryan Holmes, founder and CEO, about Hootsuite and what makes it an effective Twitter tool for business.

Shane and Steve: Why a Twitter application?

Ryan Holmes: Invoke does a lot of agency type work and created a product called Meme Labs. It's a video contesting and voting company. We use Meme Labs to help create business and brand for our clients. You can't just put up a contest, you need to drive traffic to the contest. We looked at Twitter and realized that there was no effective way for multiple users to manage one account. The other issue was that there weren't any real statistics provided by Twitter. Hootsuite was created to enable companies to have multiple users manage their brand's Twitter accounts. It also has analytics and tracking built into the suite. It turns Twitter into a manageable business tool.

Shane and Steve: What pains or challenges does it solve?

Ryan Holmes: Hootsuite as I mentioned earlier allows for a single sign on for multiple users. It also provides deep analytics that allow you to track the number of retweets you get and who is passing your message along, it allows you to pinpoint the connectors and thought leaders. With one click you can add someone to a specific group in the dashboard. For some people it provides a CRM type environment for managing their Twitter contacts. For others it's more of a content management system for managing their micro-blogging activities. It depends on your business goals. Hootsuite has a lot of applications.

Shane and Steve: How does it help companies monetize Twitter?

Ryan Holmes: Del Outlet is using Hootsuite, and they're the poster children for Twitter monetization. With a 2 or 3 person team they have generated $3 million in sales. Zappos uses it for customer relations and support. It's part of their whole corporate mix. They're using it as an extension of their entire corporate culture and brand. CEO Tony Hsieh will use Twitter to get instant feedback from his customers and staff.

With all of the analytics tools and timed tweet functions built in you can effectively do some great

A/B testing. You can compare response rates based upon the time of day, day of week, frequency, and content.

Shane and Steve: What are the important functions that Hootsuite performs?

Ryan Holmes: There are three types of 3rd party Twitter applications, they're either mobile, desktop or web based. Hootsuite is web based. Ours is backed up, and you can log on from any computer terminal in the world. Because it's web based you don't need to get your IT department to install the software. Some of the unique functionality includes pre-scheduling tweets, multi-users, RSS integration, the ability to embed your columns into 3rd party sites, and brand adoption.

Shane and Steve: What are your thoughts on social media?

Ryan Holmes: It's a buzzword right now and it's an important part of online marketing strategy. Online marketing is the umbrella, social media is one of the channels. What's being sorted out right now is exactly who owns or uses social media within the average organization. I'm thinking everyone, but that will be sorted out in time.

Yammer: Twitter for Private, Corporate Community Building

Imagine that you have 200 people working in your company or department. You don't want the whole world to see what your 200 people are doing, but you do want to create more community and synergy within and between

departments. There are often too many silos within corporations. People may feel unreachable or a bit hesitant
to approach another person they don't directly do business with on a regular basis. Yammer is a tool similar to
Twitter, but it works in a closed environment, enabling
people to project manage, update colleagues, and also
makes everybody in the corporation accessible and transparent to their co-workers.

> **Note from Stephen Jagger:** We use Yammer
> internally at Ubertor for two reasons. First, Uber-
> tor is a virtual enterprise that services thousands
> of clients yet has no office. Our staff are located
> all over the globe, including the USA, Philippines,
> Dominican Republic, and Canada. We have all
> of our team on Yammer, so that they can update
> the rest of the team instantly and constantly with
> what they are up to. This type of real time, suc-
> cinct and organization-wide communication can
> help with collaboration and solve problems. For
> example, a customer service agent may be talking
> on the phone with a client, drop a note about this
> into Yammer, and one of the programmers will see
> it and give input on a recent technical update or
> issue.
>
> We use Yammer to build the team as well. If we
> get a great testimonial via email saying how great
> a job somebody did, we will pop that into Yammer
> so the whole team can share in the success. It's be-
> come a vital tool within our business for keeping
> the lines of communication open, especially be-
> cause we are a virtual business.

Businesses that have offices with cubicles and desks
all in the same place probably need a tool like Yammer as

much as a virtual business. The marketing team is likely not talking to the programming team, which is not talking to the senior management. They are all just doing their own thing, separated in various offices or floors. Yammer can answer the question, "What are you doing?" It's an excellent way to keep the team up to date and break down traditional barriers.

Burn-out

Beyond branding, micro-blogging helps create a sense of community where it didn't exist before because of geographical or organizational barriers.

Why do people burn out? Why do entrepreneurs quit? Some people will think it's because of the long hours, others will suggest it's because of being paid less than they feel they are worth. Some people say burnout occurs from redundancy in the workplace, performing boring repetitive tasks, but what has been proven is that the number one cause for burnout in corporate America is a lack of a sense of community or no community at all whatsoever in the workplace.

Most entrepreneurs will burn out. Their motivation dies because of loneliness, as they stare at the office wall, feeling alone and disconnected from other people. Twitter will not replace human-to-human face time. Direct human contact is critical. But online contact can establish the permission to begin a relationship, and allow us to rapidly create positive connections.

Human beings are wired to connect, and tools like Yammer and Twitter are fantastic, free or nearly free tools that enable individuals that might be on their own, in another office, or another division, to stay connected to others in a meaningful way.

Chapter Eight

Social Networks

Wikipedia defines a "social network" as a structure made of nodes, which are generally individuals or organizations. They are tied by one or more interdependencies such as values, visions, ideas, financial exchange, friendship, kinship, dislike, conflict or trade.

The major online social networks include LinkedIn, Facebook, Ning, MySpace, Meetup, and Twitter, with more certain to emerge. Although we described Twitter in previous chapters as a social blogging platform, it is a social network as well. There are social bookmarking networks such as StumbleUpon, Digg, and Delicious devoted to helping you share news and links with your connections. Tumblr is another network, which is a hybrid of a blogging network and Twitter in its functionality.

The key to social networking is just that – it's sociable. It is not social spamming, it is not social direct marketing, it is not social stalking, it is social networking. It is about building relationships. There are many social networks, but for *Sociable!* we have decided to focus on the ones that have proven thus far to drive business.

MySpace was for a time the largest social network, but Facebook eclipsed it in 2008. MySpace is social but as a profitable and useful network for business it has really been on the decline and doesn't have a broad demographic like Facebook or Twitter.

Facebook, LinkedIn, Ning, Twitter, or niche-specific tools like SalesHQ.com[11], are better for driving business and revenues. There is a certain expectancy of professionalism as well as marketing occurring at a tolerable level on these networks.

Facebook

Facebook has over 250 million active users[12] and growing globally. Two Harvard students founded it as a tool for students to post information on themselves and connect with fellow alumni. It was expanded to other schools, and then rapidly rolled out into mainstream North America and then globally.

It allows you to connect with people from your past, and people that you are presently socializing or doing business with. It allows you to keep people in your network up to date on what you are doing, and vice versa. If used properly you can do this very efficiently.

Multiple Channels, Multiple Mediums

Facebook allows you to update people on what you're doing using multiple mediums and channels. Some people like photos, others like brief notes, some want to see what other people are saying about you and your business.

Instead of you pushing out all your information, people can consume as much or as little information as they want, as they browse your profile. People can choose to read a brief update or dig deeper to see photos of your last VIP event, or what your friends and associates have written about you or shared with you.

---

11   SalesHQ.com is a sales professional specific social networking site

12   Statistic from http://www.facebook.com/press/info.php?statistics

Using Facebook is like being able at any time to jump into a networking function with the hundreds of people that you are connected with around the world. You can immediately start a conversation with your entire network and get to see what they are up to in real time.

Here a few of the things that you can do with Facebook to enhance your business:

1. Keep up to date on what your contacts are doing. In the past, without tools like this, it would almost be impossible to see what the hundreds of people you know are up to on a regular basis. Today, you can do it instantly.

2. Reconnect to people with whom you have lost contact.

3. Plan and manage the invitations to an event.

4. Post videos or link to YouTube videos or Viddler videos.

5. Research prospects and browse corporate pages to develop dialogue with clients and prospects.

6. Forge relationships with other members by commenting on their photos, notes, videos, and status updates.

7. Purchase advertising and send targeted messages to people in specific demographics, geographical locations, or even by specific search terms or things they are talking about at that moment.

8. Build a corporate page showcasing your services, products, and events.

9. Add the feed from your blog, so that every time you update your blog, everyone on your Facebook network is notified.

There are a few precautions we would like to mention. Too many people post inappropriate material on Facebook that can harm their career, privacy or even loved ones. This can be a generational issue. What generation Y or millennials feel is appropriate public behavior on the internet is not going to be seen the same way by baby boomers or Gen X'ers. Content you post on your Facebook profile may be acceptable within your circle of close friends, but one has to realize that clients, business colleagues and corporate recruiters who use Facebook for background checks are going to scrutinize your behavior. So it makes sense to be careful about what you post.

We have probably broken most of the rules listed below learning to use Facebook. Don't make the same mistakes. Here are some quick tips to make Facebook work, and also make it safe for you and your corporation:

1. Behave yourself in public. Behave as if everyone owns a videophone and a computer. If what you do in public is interesting enough, weird enough or loud enough, it is going to end up on the internet and probably on Facebook. Expect other people to hear about it.

2. Never post information that can be used to steal your identity. This includes your mother's maiden name, the year you were born, your home address or anything else that could give someone potential access to your credit report, banking or citizenship information.

3. Don't be a troll. Trolls don't live under bridges anymore. In today's context, a troll

refers to someone who is malicious, hurtful or just plain mean. There is no place for that offline or online for anyone who wants to build a strong personal brand. Your goal is community building and being a thought leader. Being a troll is just the opposite. If someone is wrong, we have to find a positive way to interact with and bring them onside. We will talk more about trolls later in chapter 10.

4. This is not a business topic, but it is important to think about. Don't put pictures of your children in publicly accessible folders. It opens up an area of danger, exposing them to all kinds of risks. Make sure to set your privacy settings accordingly, allowing access only to trusted friends and family.

5. Don't make it all professional. Do post pictures of your latest holiday. Do post information about your friends and family and what you are doing (keeping in mind safety of course). Let people see all sides of you and they can determine what information they want to digest.

6. It is okay for people to see you holding a beer. Many people delete those types of photos on Facebook, because they don't want their customers or potential customers to see them with alcohol. People know that cocktail parties happen, and know that business occurs in these types of environments, as long as you are respectable in

what you are doing. Your target market and community will help dictate what is appropriate for you and your business.

7. We have mentioned this in many parts of this book already, but stop selling and start sharing and contributing. If you are constantly pushing marketing messages people are going to disengage or delete you. Find ways to engage others and promote what they are doing, and you will find they will gladly promote you in return.

Be authentic

Know that your public behavior is going to be well known because in today's digital age, it is going to end up online. So, you know what? If you make claims to certain behaviors or standards, and then are found in breach of them, your reputation will suffer damage. To put it simply, don't be hypocritical. This should go without saying. To some degree, if you are upfront about who you are and what you believe in, and you wear it on your sleeve, there are enough people in the social networks to connect with and generate business from. It is when you are presenting one face publicly and a different face privately that these tools come back to bite you in the end.

We have to laugh at (yes, we're laughing at you not with you) Facebook profiles that only feature professionally done photography such as an airbrushed over-coifed sales person or business owner leaning on a Corinthian pillar. That's not being sociable or transparent, that's 1980. Where are the impromptu networking pictures, the candid office shots and the great office Halloween party pics? Yes have some professional pictures, but also show a bit more of your personal human side.

How about a Facebook profile for business and then one for who I really am?

We are often asked if one can have separate personal and business Facebook profiles. We believe you shouldn't do that. Sure, it can be set up, but there is nothing to stop people from loading photos of an event into their account and tagging your personal profile when you would have wanted them to tag your business profile. You can untag yourself, but somebody else will tag you again. It is something you can't control. So, the guiding principle is just be a good person, don't do things you don't want people to see.

We've heard people say, "I am not on Facebook." Our response to them is always, "Yes, you are. It's just you that can't see yourself on Facebook." A friend could go to your child's birthday party, take photos and post them on Facebook, and you would not be able to see or stop this if you're not engaged online. Keep in mind that while you should try to avoid it as best you can, you can't stop it.

N⊙ISE TO SIGNAL
RobCottingham.ca

On Facebook, 273 people know I'm a dog.
The rest can only see my limited profile.

Who is your company's brand leader?

Your staff are posting data, photos, and writing opinions on your company. As a CEO, if you are not involved in social media, but your staff is, you have a lower chance of directing the brand and fostering professionalism. However, if you are online, connected to your staff, your customers, your distributors, your family and friends, you are contributing to those communities and building a strong network. Ideally, you should be using tools like Twitter and your blog to drive people from one platform to another. The key message here is it is all about being *Sociable!* and, of course, reputation and brand management, and you can't do it by being passive, by lurking in the back. You have to be proactive. This gives you the highest chance of managing your reputation in a positive way.

What do you update on your Facebook status?

Update your status every once in a while, probably much less than you do on Twitter. Talk about what you are up to, where you are, what events you will be attending. An update once a day will often suffice.

> **Note from Stephen Jagger:** I am a big fan of uploading photos from events and ensuring that I tag the people in the photos, because those photos will show up on their profiles. This provides a way for you to show who you are, what you do, and the events you attend. The whole idea is having more of the Facebook community see and learn about things you do. Every video I post I also add to Facebook. As a rule, to create good PR, I will add the link to major media news articles in which I am referenced, as this allows my connections to understand what I do in my work and why they might want to learn more about Reachd, Outsourcing Things Done, and Ubertor. Sure, they watch my videos and see the types of events I put on, and what kind of business I do from viewing my Facebook profile, but it just puts it over the top to see a major newspaper article or TV interview on that same topic. It is a great way to add some more impact to your profile online.

Connect to People You Meet Offline Using Facebook

If you are at a trade show or similar event, try politely asking the people you meet if you could take their picture, making sure you get their business cards. Instead of just uploading all these photos to your corporate site, upload them to Facebook as well, and tag the individuals. All their friends and the business associates connected to them will see they have been tagged in a photo at your event. They will visit the picture, and perhaps the rest of the album, and in many cases will add themselves to your fans page or begin to follow you on Facebook because of their interest or the implied endorsement by their friends. Check with your local laws and guidelines to see if you require permission to do this. In some regions simply posting a notice on your website and event tickets that photos will be taken and used will suffice, in other regions or circumstances you may require written permission.

A lot of professional speakers, event organizers and trade show organizers are now using Facebook to passively promote themselves. Facebook is not a social networking tool to be overlooked. It offers many social media and social networking tools for free with over 250 million users with whom you can potentially connect.

LinkedIn

LinkedIn allows you to search for leads within your current business network, to expand your network, and provide and request endorsements. LinkedIn also offers status updates just like Facebook and Twitter. It is a very powerful tool and is a great place as a professional to start if Facebook is a bit intimidating for you.

Some people have referred to Linkedin as Facebook for adults. It is much more limited as far as the scope of what you can upload, what you can say to other people or who you can contact. This can actually be a positive thing. It's a vehicle for well-networked and credible people joining networks with other people they trust and would endorse. This intent makes an introduction on LinkedIn a powerful means of connecting with new contacts. LinkedIn has a wide reach, with member across the globe, including executives from all Fortune 500 companies.

LinkedIn predates Facebook and Twitter, yet has fewer members than Facebook. It is a highly professional online social networking and referral generation system. Corporate recruiters regularly use LinkedIn to find new recruits and to check backgrounds of job candidates. It is more like a personal CV or résumé online, but it is dynamic. You can update it with your activities, and other people connected to you on LinkedIn can write endorsements for you.

Your LinkedIn profile should include your latest achievements, your work history, your biography, and a personal photo. LinkedIn has expanded further into the social media space by allowing you to import blog feeds. It has integrated with Google Docs and a tool called Slide Share, which enable to upload and share Power Point files with your network.

You can search through the people associated with your own contacts for prospects or potential business partners you may want to make new connections with. Once found, you make a request to be introduced by the mutual connection linking you with the prospect.

LinkedIn is set up to ensure you only invite people you are willing to endorse, so that people can't just go into your network and say, "Hey! I want to meet Stephen Jagger because I am connected to Shane Gibson." Typically people on LinkedIn have fewer connections than they would on Facebook or Twitter, but those connections tend to be more professional, and are people they want to endorse.

While it is possible to directly add someone you don't know without having his or her contact details, there is a risk in doing this. If even a small number of people respond by clicking the "I don't know this person" button, LinkedIn will either limit your ability to use their system or ban you all together.

One of the best ways to make new connections on LinkedIn is to begin to join some of the groups and participate in the "Answers" section where people ask business questions. You can reply to them, and begin to generate meaningful dialogue with other business professionals in various industries.

Ning.com – A White Labeled Network to Build Your Own Community

Ning.com enables you to create your own social network for anything. It's like having a small Facebook or LinkedIn community just for you and your contacts. You can create a social network for knitting enthusiasts, insurance agents, project management professionals, or you could create a social network for people who are really into certain authors.

Because you are essentially creating a networking and collaboration platform using the Ning system, you set the tone for the level and type of interaction that occurs. It can either be very business orientated and professional or it can be very social, and non-businesslike. You can either use the system at yourdomain.com or pick a web address and extension something.ning.com and create a closed community or very focused part of your social network where you can discuss common interests.

If you have a significantly sized network, Ning enables you to build a little bit more of a fence around your community. It lets you approve members and direct the level of interaction that occurs. From a corporate perspective, it enables you to further brand the network over and above what the other tools will allow. You have a fair bit more autonomy with what goes on within your own network than you do within other networks. As the creator and sponsor of the platform you will often be able to influence or even set the mood for social etiquette, interaction and the level of marketing (or lack thereof) that goes on.

One good example of an organization that has used Ning really well to build a community is Interchanges.com. They are the creators of InSocialMedia.com. We were fortunate enough to be able to interview the CEO and Founder Chris Patterson recently. Here's the interview:

> Shane and Steve: How long have you been in the online branding and marketing space and how have social media and networking changed things?

> Chris Patterson: I started working with American Online in the mid 90s. The paradigm shift from the early web to web2.0 has been tremendously disruptive to traditional marketing. With the opportunity to have interactive communication via the web with no boundaries for growth lends an immense opportunity to companies that embrace this new medium.

> Shane and Steve: What kinds of companies and projects do you work on in social media?

Chris Patterson: We've worked with companies like Snapple, Energizer and Kanye West to help them increase their brand exposure and develop stronger relationships. What's even more exciting is how we can help even the smallest of businesses gain quick and significant awareness to help grow their businesses as well.

Shane and Steve: Creating and hosting a space like InSocialMedia.com is a large endeavor. What were the strategic reasons for doing this?

Chris Patterson: We simply love the space and all the amazing minds that are "in social media." We wanted to provide a place where people could engage, interact and learn together. Furthermore, we realized early on that having a brain trust of experts and enthusiasts at InSocialMedia would be invaluable to serve our network of friends and customers.

Shane and Steve: Where did most of your InSocialMedia.com members come from?

Chris Patterson: Initially we began to do influencer outreach and invited our "heroes" like Gary Vaynerchuk, Julia Roy and of course Shane Gibson to be a part of our community. Once we had some well-respected experts in the community the word quickly spread through Twitter, Facebook, blogs and others.

Shane and Steve: What made you choose Ning. com as the platform to build your community on?

Chris Patterson: Ning was simply the easiest and fastest community to deploy. We've been very pleased with the platform.

Shane and Steve: Any advice for organizations looking at using Ning.com to build a community and social network?

Chris Patterson: While I think it is important to think out a plan of action for what your community will be, it's much more important to take action. Start with a concept, begin to build the network and then you can always change directions along the way. Ready. Shoot. Aim.

Shane and Steve: Any advice for brands, people and companies that are new to the social media and networking space?

Chris Patterson: The biggest barrier for entry to brands, people and companies that we have seen has been a lack of education and analysis paralysis. Something simple that anyone can do is set a goal to study and learn just one social media platform per month. You will be amazed at the opportunities and influence you can grow in just one year.

Meetup.com

Meetup.com is like no other social networking site. Its sole purpose is to get those who network online to connect in person. The "About Us" page on their website summarizes it well:

"Meetup is the world's largest network of local groups. Meetup makes it easy for anyone to organize a local group or find one of the thousands already meeting up face-to-face. More than 2,000 groups get together in local communities each day, each one with the goal of improving themselves or their communities.

Meetup's mission is to revitalize local community and help people around the world self-organize. Meetup believes that people can change their personal world, or the whole world, by organizing themselves into groups that are powerful enough to make a difference"

We promote Meetup.com events using Twitter, Facebook, LinkedIn and YouTube. We have also live stream events on the web via video using Ustream.tv. If used properly all of these tools can work synergistically and speak to several target audiences and demographics.

Meetup.com allows you to pull together people you network with online and get them to collaborate, share best practices and connect in person. It costs less than $100 per year to register and organize a Meetup.com group on any topic area that you choose. We operate four major Meetup groups in Vancouver and Toronto, and they are one of our least expensive but most effective tools for marketing and generating word-of-mouth business.

Interview Scott Heiferman CEO and Co-founder of Meetup

We had the opportunity to connect with Scott Heiferman, CEO and co-founder of Meetup. According to Scott, Meetup was originally developed to help organize and promote large tech community events and soirees, and is now growing at a breakneck pace of 500,000 new members a month.

They have even caught the eye of the White House. Scott and a small group of other leaders that help communities to self-organize and create positive change were hosted by the White House to learn of the Obama administration's vision and to collaborate and share ideas. Meetup is facilitating the creation of change and community across the globe.

Scott shared with us that Meetup's purpose was to "use the internet to get off the internet" and that it was about the "growth of the local community group." As a true social technology leader, Scott hasn't pushed his vision of what Meetup should be or do for its members. Here's what Scott had to say:

"The vision for Meetup is driven by how people are using it. It's driven by what people need. What if there was a local community group everywhere about everything? Building capacity in the community, [you can] have people that are passionate about something, or even diagnosed with something, and there's a group there when they need it."

When we asked him what makes Meetup different than other social networking platforms here's what he had to say:

"You have different pieces of your life, Facebook is for friends and family, LinkedIn for your professional life, Twitter for when you want to broadcast to and connect with the world. We all have something that is important to us that our friends, professional circle, and family can't support us in. Meetup can be the solution. That's the role of a community group. Every town has always needed these types of local groups. We are reinventing how it happens in the 21st century."

Lastly Scott provided some insight and advice to would-be Meetup organizers:

"When you create real community with the right intentions you are creating a lot of value that can be shared by everyone. A lot of that gets reflected back on the organizers. Everyone has something to teach. Mom Meetups are the biggest demographic, for instance, sharing potty training knowledge, better than any book or magazine. People turning to each other.

"As an organizer, proactively seek out what members are trying to get out of something. Don't be afraid just to ask. Throw it out there. Don't presume. Find ways to ask people what they are trying to get out of it. Your community can help you build a successful group.

"Lastly, don't be afraid to ask people to take on roles and responsibilities. Get the interdependency between people going on."

Scott's overall message and vision is that the most successful Meetup groups are the ones where many people have ownership in the direction and topics. Good Meetup organizers create value and get members engaged through collaborative leadership. All of this value creation and genuine community building can only help you build a strong *Sociable!* brand.

Think Long-term When Social Networking

A lot of sales professionals, when they get on these types of networks and see a list of people, think, "Oh! Great. This is another list like a directory I bought. I am just going to hammer it, cold call it or cold spam it and see if out of a thousand people if I can get ten to buy something."

This is absolutely the quickest way to get blacklisted in any social network. Instead, we need to develop relationships and conversations. If you are just joining LinkedIn, uploading your contact base, then asking for their connections, and pitching everybody within the first week, you have already lost.

Think long term and ask, "How can I build a following or a strong reputation to ensure that I become trustworthy?" Remember, your goal with these social networks is not to get referrals. Your goal is to become referable, to become credible, and to build a following through value added interactions. Doing this well will create an endless stream of contacts. In good time they will be knocking on your door, wanting to do business with you.

Leveraged Networking

When all you had in the past was a fax machine and a phone, most people had a hard time just keeping up to date on their top 30 clients and what was happening in their lives. If you wanted to keep a client base of 500 people up to date on what you were doing it would involve time and resource intensive direct mail campaigns.

Today by using a combination of Facebook, LinkedIn, Twitter and Meetup you can monitor and stay in touch with thousands of people with very little upfront cost. Invest some effort in building your network this way and in a short period of time you will find you have a significant presence and momentum within your target markets.

Chapter Nine

Social Media Etiquette

Within every social group there are unique protocols. We both played rugby growing up. There were certain expected traditions and behaviors on and off the field. When we decided to take up golf we had to learn a whole new etiquette in order to be accepted and gain rapport with the other golfers.

In rugby we would all yell when we were going for the ball, but in golf you're silent when anyone is hitting the ball. In rugby tearing up the field is a sign you played a good game, in golf you if you don't replace your divots you could be banned from the course and never invited again by your clients to play in their tournament.

This is a chapter that we know belongs in the book, but one that we struggle with nonetheless. This is because we recognize that adherence to social norms, even in social media, is required for all of us to get along reasonably well. Yet, we also understand that it is sometimes those who meet with entrepreneurial success are ones able to think and behave a little more freely, shall we say.

This is a little bit of a pet peeve for us, it's a chapter that we have in this book that we almost don't agree with. We consider ourselves outliers in the business space, people who don't quite fit to the norm and actually are somewhat opposed to structure and people telling us what to do as entrepreneurs.

Social media has many types of playing fields and expected behaviors. In any social structure there is behavior deemed necessary in order to be to be part of the crowd. What does a leader have to do? What does their behavior look like? We wonder if some of the rules are put in place designed to stratify the networks and to limit the growth of newbies to the benefit of the early adopters. When do we break the rules? When do we adhere to them? This is difficult to answer, as we that know sometimes the most successful people in an industry are the ones that break the rules.

Social Etiquette vs. Business Etiquette

Let's compare business etiquette to social etiquette. Depending upon your target market there will be a set of offline rules that are going to pour online to some degree. Within certain groups, business groups or otherwise, there will be an accepted social norm or behavior that's promoted. We have to be very careful at limiting ourselves, but at the same time we can take certain actions online that blow up in our face and destroy our brand. As we stated earlier, sometimes we need to break the rules, be a little edgy or take a risk to win. With that said, we also need to be prepared for the downside.

The Motrin Debacle

A good example would be the Motrin Moms debacle that occurred in 2008. The makers of the painkiller Motrin created what they felt was a very tongue in cheek video and published on their website. The video supposed to be humorous, making light of being a mom. It accused mothers of trying to be fashionable by carrying their children on their side in sling like apparatuses, and talked about how Motrin could help them.

It enraged thousands of mom bloggers and erupted in the Twittersphere as outrage. People felt like they were considering children a fashion accessory and calling their mothers shallow and conceited. Being clever with social media blew up in their face.

After the Motrin Moms issue erupted, it became obvious that Motrin was not monitoring online chatter to stay on top of their brand. Worse than them saying the wrong thing was the fact they didn't know there was any response yet. There were thousands of responses on Twitter, on blogs, on YouTube, yet Motrin kept mum for almost a day. In fact, it got to the point where the traffic volume hitting their website allegedly crashed their servers. Some suggested that not knowing how to respond, Motrin just turned off their website until they could regroup and figure out what they could do. They also tried to remove all evidence of these videos. They eventually apologized.

Things can go wrong extremely fast. It is important to understand social media etiquette, what to say, what to avoid saying. Realize that even if you're doing the right thing and creating a following, you could offend some people. The most important thing is how quickly you respond if this occurs.

Here are some of the social media norms violated by Motrin:

Rule #1 Social Media is about listening.

They were not actively listening for feedback and were unaware of the negative spin on their brand. Although the video was up for only one evening, a single evening of negative spin in the social media space can damage a brand for a long time.

Rule #2 If something goes amiss, respond quickly.

There is an expectation in the social media space for brands to respond to questions and concerns in a quick and personal manner. Motrin failed to do this.

Rule #3 If you're wrong admit it and don't hide your mistakes.

The social media community can be forgiving. Admit your mistakes and you're usually okay. Motrin reacted to negativity by deleting the video and allegedly attempted to remove evidence of their blunder well before even apologizing. This lack of transparency, a desire to hide an error, is considered a faux pas for most in the social media space. By doing this they actually lost control because people had grabbed the video and uploaded it to YouTube. People didn't need to go to Motrin.com to see the video and Motrin lost all capacity to get into the conversation at that point.

Using Social Media for Business

There are a lot of things that you can think about when considering social media etiquette. There are many subjects, such as politics, religion, race, pro-union, non-union, that can tweak your readers or your followers in a good or a bad way, and it's up to you to decide what makes the most sense for you.

Realize that You're Now On Stage 24 Hours a Day

A decade ago, it wouldn't have been proper to take pictures of your clients at a party, publish them in a magazine without their permission, and then distribute it to hundreds people. Today, people get their pictures taken at events all the time and uploaded into Facebook or

Flickr. It has become a social media norm. Social media is changing the etiquette, which can vary as we move from network to network.

Some people will say you shouldn't talk too much about your personal life on Twitter. Others will say you shouldn't talk about business too much on Twitter. And there are some suggesting that you shouldn't be always promoting your blog posts. As social media evolves and its demographics shift we will also see an evolution of social media etiquette.

Often, early adopters with a large influence push their opinions on the rest of us. It is just their opinion, it's not etiquette. There are networks within the networks with various social norms. You have to decide whom you want to attract, and ensure that your behavior is acceptable to your target market.

Commenting on Blogs

There are some social networking and social media basics that we have to adhere to if we want to avoid the wrath of the larger social media community. Blogs are your home base, so when you visit someone's blog, you're in their space. The level of professionalism demonstrated by the blogger should tell you what type of comments you should be leaving on their blog.

We firmly believe you should identify yourself. Many people will leave anonymous comments, but we're not big fans of it. If you live in Iran or China and you're making anti-government comments as a way to exercise free speech, then we understand that being anonymous is going to keep you alive and out of jail. If you're a financial advisor in Texas commenting on another business blog, there's no real need to hide your identity. Unless you can't back up what you're saying. In that case, the solution would be to not comment at all.

When you comment, identify yourself by first and last name, with a link to your website, so people can learn more about you. This goes towards the notion of engaging the community in greater dialogue, by inviting people to get to know you and respond to you. It's the opposite of hiding behind anonymity. Whether they like or dislike your opinion, at least they can have a little peek to see who is making that statement. And don't just comment for the sake of getting your link in somebody else's blog, you are just going to annoy the blog owner and get deleted. Make a comment that adds value to the discussion. Strong comments can begin a spin-off dialogue, either on the original site, or sometimes back on your own, if you have provided a link back.

Comments on Your Blog

Comments on your own blog present an opportunity for you to have a conversation. However, you have an advantage in that you have a certain degree of control over the conversation. You have the ability to add more comments, stop the commenting, or even edit or delete comments if you choose.

The etiquette around editing comments is important. While you can delete a comment you are not happy about if it's offensive or excessively negative, editing somebody else's text is not acceptable.

Provide a Platform for Your Customer to Brand You

Remember, your customers own your brand. You need to provide them opportunity to talk about it. If they can't comment about your brand on your blog, they are going to do it elsewhere, perhaps on Facebook or Twitter or someone else's blog, where you can't get involved in the conversation as readily.

A primary goal of the comments is to provide your audience with an avenue to create feedback. But it can, and we believe should, be a two way conversation. So when someone makes a comment on your blog, make an effort to respond. It can further the conversation. It's bad etiquette not to allow comments, or some other avenue for feedback.

Some people will include their email address when they comment on your blog. After you respond to them, try sending them a quick email saying, "By the way, thanks for your comment on my blog. I have responded to it." This may draw them back again to re-comment.

Keep Your Channels Open

If you have a blog, keep your comments open. Several content management systems have plug-ins to limit spam comment postings. These plug-in utilities recognize and delete any comments that are made in less than five seconds of someone reaching your page. It will also delete anything on the IP blacklist, which is a catalog of addresses of well known spam robots.

Are You a Twit or a Twitterer?

At the time of writing this book, Twitter was in the middle of a 1600% growth explosion in user base, from mid 2008 to mid 2009. Yet we also know that Twitter could disappear within a year or two of publishing. These rules are about micro-blogging etiquette or social network etiquette in general, but we'll use Twitter as our working example.

Who Do You Follow?

Some people say you should follow back everyone that is following you on Twitter or Stumbleupon, and others say you should just follow the people you are interested in listening to. We would advise you to not follow back everybody that follows you. Certainly don't feel obliged to follow Twitter spammers. They are easy to spot. Their updates are usually about a miracle cure, winning a free computer, or getting rich without working. They will also be only updating about themselves and often will be following 2000 people but only have 50 or 100 following them back.

Imagine you're a successful business person or a pastor or a school teacher and someone looks down the list of people you are following and sees that you're following a well known racist or extremely offensive political pundit. Game over. Don't follow anyone before you check them out. Following someone can be perceived as an endorsement or vote of confidence in that individual.

Don't worry about following people that follow you. It's okay if you are following more or less people than are following you. It's just a matter of following the people that make sense to you because their comments are of interest to you.

Social media is also a business intelligence tool. Follow your customers and your competitors even if they make a lot of noise and are uninteresting.. This goes beyond just etiquette, it helps you keep up to date.

No Generic Auto-Replies

An auto-reply is a method of sending an automatic "Thank-you for following me" type message to your new followers on Twitter. Auto-reply tools are provided by third party software such as Tweetlater. We would strongly suggest you avoid using them.

In a recent study done on Twitip.com, more than 1000 Twitter users were polled and over 80% reported that they either "hated" or "unfollowed" people who sent automated direct messages on Twitter.

Write in a Way That Ensures You Can't be Misunderstood

Keep in mind that Twitter gives you only 140 characters, which is not much room to make a point. It's also just text, so sarcasm or humor may not come through. If members of your audience don't know your personality, they may not know if you are being sarcastic, funny or serious, so you have to be careful and consider your post from the point of view of a person that doesn't know you very well. You don't want to offend somebody because you wrote something that you thought was funny, and your close friends would think is funny, but comes across in the wrong way.

Once You Hit Send, It's All Over

It is so easy to hit the send button, but do realize you can never take back a sent email, tweet, or comment on a blog. Comments can be found in Twitter Search for some time after being deleted. Another concern is that a tweet doesn't just go to one person, it's there for the whole world to see, for better or for worse. Someone could easily screen capture it and post it to their blog or share it in other ways.

Ask Permission

If you take a few photos with others, ask if it's okay to post some pictures online. It may be expected or accepted that photos taken at a public function like Meetup will be posted automatically, but if you are at a more private, social function, it is appropriate to ask for permission. Either gain their consent while you are snapping the pictures, or send them a quick email to tell them you have event photos that you would like to upload to and would like their permission to proceed.

What's In A Name?

Pseudonyms, nick names or short names are acceptable if you are going to use Facebook or other networks for social purposes only. However, your business associates may start to wonder why you are using a false name. Does this guy have a secret life? Does he have a separate profile? Why is he able to see everything about my life, but he is hiding parts of himself from me?

In our experience people who are more transparent and work on their overall behavior offline and online, versus trying to shroud their identity, are more successful.

Facebook Apps Can Kill Credibility

Resist the temptation to use most Facebook 3rd party applications. Most of these apps add to your noise but don't add value. We have seen them all:

> Poker
> Sexual IQ
> Throw a Snowball
> Auction Your Friend
> Adopt a Virtual Poodle

All of these types of applications have nothing to do with adding value or gaining trust in your network. Every time you update your activity, your network will hear about how many poodles you have groomed, how many snowballs you got hit with or how low your sexual IQ has become. This is not how to brand and build community. If you're shaking your head right now and wondering what we're talking about, not to worry. Just heed this warning, so that when someone invites you to install one of these apps, hit the button that says "ignore" and never look back.

LinkedIn Etiquette

LinkedIn is a site where you must be transparent. If you forget to mention that you worked somewhere or overstate a role with a client or a previous employer it's not like padding an individual resume, it's worse because it can be seen by thousands of people. Also the contacts who know you can see the exaggeration and will most likely distance themselves from you. It's like being the guy at social functions who stretches the truth or takes credit for other people's work. People may not directly confront you, but this bad etiquette will have you being invited to fewer events.

Your associations can reflect back upon you, so be discerning about whom you accept as a connection on LinkedIn. Also be careful about whom you endorse, and whom you ask to endorse you.

Making Contact in LinkedIn

LinkedIn provides users the ability to indicate whether or not they are willing to be contacted directly, or only via a mutual link. Attempting to make direct contact with someone who doesn't welcome it is not a good idea, even if you manage to dig up their email address. LinkedIn provides an option to say, "I don't know this person" and LinkedIn will actually begin to limit your ability to connect with people. In addition you may have ruined what could have been a good contact. The better approach is to see if the contacts you do have are linked or connected to your intended target. Often it is only two or three contacts away. Write a nice message to be passed along through the network on your behalf.

Take your time. It takes longer on LinkedIn to build up a base of connections than it does with Twitter or Facebook, but you can get some very powerful business introductions if you use it properly.

Cultural Etiquette

If your network spreads beyond your immediate cultural domain, you need to consider that social norms will differ around the world. This is a challenge, especially because social media permeates through all geographies, cultures and age groups. Understand the formalities and privacy issues that are respected in other cultures. Certain behaviors are not as appropriate in one country as another. This book is not about cross cultural awareness, but realize that's also going to play into your etiquette depending upon where you are networking globally.

The Speed of the Leader Determines the Pace of the Pack

The pace set by early adopters and how they use a particular social media platform is going to influence how it is used by the majority of people that follow along and join in the network. Facebook was originally designed for university students, allowing them to publicly post information and photos about themselves and their friends. This is still the social norm.

Twitter

The rules and the etiquette behind Twitter came from the earlier adopters. The system was originally intended as a micro-blogging platform but morphed into a social networking and communications tool because of the way early adopters used it. Twitter is a platform where it's socially acceptable to follow or connect with people you hardly know, and you're not expected to respond to every message sent to you. In contrast, ignoring a message on LinkedIn or an email or blog comment would be bad etiquette in most cases.

Meetup.com

Meetup.com has its own set of social norms. If people are choosing to be part of the Meetup that we have created, it does give the group founders the ability to push a little bit of their product or service to those people within the Meetup. Depending on what type of Meetup, people see it as part of being a member.

> **Note from Stephen Jagger:** I run a real estate technology Meetup. It's attended by realtors and mortgage brokers coming to a monthly Meetup to learn about real estate technology. These events are free and my companies Ubertor and Reachd organize and fund the Meetup events. From the inception of this group there was always some pitching and direct messages from Ubertor and Reachd, and the members don't tend to complain. I set a standard from the beginning. The membership understands that they will benefit from the meetings, and that the entrance fee is to hear us occasionally promote our services.

Our Vancouver Sales Performance Meetup is just about the opposite. When we formed it, one of the things we decided was to have members "Leave your pitch at the door." We decided very early on that the group was about sharing best practices, connecting, and that relationships would evolve business organically. The purpose was to empower one another, not to sell or pitch. The first few times some people didn't quite get it, but after a while, once we got a critical mass of 80 to 100 members that would attend, the group able to self police and abide by the mandate. People came to understand very quickly it was an open, proactive group and there was no pitching. The founders established this social etiquette.

If attend a similar meeting elsewhere, we often find a higher level of pitching and brochure-ware coming out, and people actually giving their elevator pitch to each other for an hour before they begin their networking. The best thing you can do is observe how the leaders and influencers behave, as a good initial gauge of what is acceptable.

Or You Can Just Break All the Rules

We started our own Meetup groups when other people in the city were already having real estate and sales events because we wanted to create our own groups, with their own unique culture and etiquette. The goal is to find people that resonate with your leadership style and respond to your message.

We admitted earlier that we have broken most of these rules discussed here, everything from posting unsatisfactory photos to spam commenting on other people's blogs. We weren't being malicious or stupid, we were simply traveling in uncharted territory and learning as we went along. We have also suffered the consequences. The reality, however, is if you sound and act like everyone else, you're not a thought leader, so in most cases you may have to push the limits of etiquette to move ahead of the pack.

The observations we have shared in this chapter are just that, observations. We don't make the rules, but we do try to observe them. Sometimes you have to bend or break the rules to get ahead, but you also have to be prepared for the backlash.

It's important sometimes to break the rules, to be that early adopter and thought leader. As long as the payoff is big and you can live with the downside, you may want to do it.

Chapter Ten

Trolls, Naysayers, and the Crowd

Negative Feedback is Part of Being Successful

In his book *Failing Forward: Turning Mistakes into Stepping Stones for Success,* John Maxwell talks about the fact that failure is not the opposite of success, it's actually part of the process of becoming successful. Failure is actually feedback. If you are not pushing hard and trying new and innovative things, you probably will never fail, but you also will most likely not reach a level of great success. If you have momentum, momentum creates friction. As you grow a following, as your message proliferates throughout your network, you will have a certain level of negative feedback. How you respond to it will determine your level of social media success.

To be a leader in the social media sphere, you must open yourself up to the masses. In doing so, there can be a risk of being misunderstood or misquoted, receiving negative feedback, and even of failure. However, we have discovered that in using social media, sometimes being safe is actually not safe.

If you always play it safe, take no risks, and don't push the envelope, you will be seen as a grey brand that is not doing anything exciting. It's better to be pushing the limits, pushing the envelope, pushing the rules, finding that line and crossing it. Be seen as a thought leader and people will start to follow you, and your business will grow. Pushing the limits is about putting forward thought provoking ideas, being more generous than your competitors think is practical, or even taking a stand on contentious issue.

With that come the trolls, trouble makers and naysayers. There will always be people with an opinion opposite to your own. There is always going to be somebody writing in their blog disagreeing with you. There is always going to be somebody in Twitter claiming that what you are saying is incorrect or misguided. You just have to not worry about those people. Yes address it, but see it as part of your social media activities. Anyone being bold will have opposition. If you are confident in what you are doing and saying then you can get involved in those conversations, respond to them, and move forward.

N⊙ISE TO SIGNAL
RobCottingham.ca

So what do you say we go to my place after school and hound celebrities off the Internet?

Anonymous Critics

There are times when we wouldn't suggest following up or commenting on what people have to say. If the naysayers, the trouble makers and the trolls are anonymous, realize that they are not confident in their position, that's why they are hiding. It doesn't merit a response. Hit delete, block, or unfollow as necessary and don't give them the attention that they are craving. Don't be drawn in to responding to anonymous comments or anonymous blogs, just ignore them. In our opinion in order to merit attention or a response you have to at least identify who you are. Imagine conducting a seminar and having a member of the audience with a paper bag on their head hurl questions at you. They don't deserve a response.

Never Fight With a Pig

Peter Thomas, founder of Century 21 Canada wrote a great book a number of years back called "Never Fight With a Pig". You never fight with a pig because pigs like to get dirty, get in the mud, and roll around in their own excrement. That's what trolls are, they are pigs! Go back to our purpose, which is to contribute to community, be a valued resource and a trusted advisor. How could rolling around the mud with the troll do that for you?

Anybody who is worthwhile having as a follower on your mission or your movement is probably someone who is not going to listen to the trolls anyway.

Some People May Be Mean But They Might Be Right

Troublemakers are people who instigate, people who are poking holes and looking for negative things but they are not necessarily all trolls. They actually might identify themselves, but their personality is one of being a mismatcher. These types of people always look at what could be wrong with something. Their approach is one of the devil's advocate.

When asked for their opinion, they actually don't know, all they know is their opinion is going to be the opposite of the consensus view at any point. These people may be worth a response.

The best way to engage them is to state your opinion, then thank them for their difference of opinion and their feedback. Sometimes our critics are our best teachers, they help us sharpen our business model. Often for every vocal critic there are dozens of people who feel the same way but don't express it.

We can tend to see everyone who criticizes us as the enemy and all those who support us as friends. Sometimes real friends are people who have nothing to gain but will risk the relationship in order to let us know we're off base or wrong. Those that always agree with us may have ulterior motives. Be wary of your ego online. The rant you post in response to a critic will be there forever.

Negative Customer Feedback is Also Part of Your Brand

An upset customer can undo a lot of hard work we have put into building our brand and trustworthiness. They can be your anti-brand. If an unhappy customer arrives at your website, it is not an opportunity to call them a troll. If they have identified themselves and taken the time to tell you something it's a chance for you to engage them, solve the problem and create an advocate. If you solve someone's problem in a public forum it actually becomes a positive brand building activity.

Use it As a Branding Opportunity

Scott Monty, head of social media at Ford, talks about the company's brand to supporters and naysayers, happy and unhappy customers alike. He searches Twitter, blogs, and other social media platforms and appears to be on the internet all day, looking for comments that are negative or misdirected thoughts and about the Ford Motor Company.

Instead of threatening them like a traditional organization with legal action, he engages. He will spot comments on Twitter or a blog that say something like "Ford doesn't care about the environment." He will quickly jump in sharing links to Ford's green manufacturing processes and improvements in fuel efficiency and emissions standards. He engages people and educates them. Scott turns negative feedback or naysayers into branding opportunities.

Do Your Homework and Know Your Business

Scott is well studied in what's going on in the company, in the manufacturing policies, and what's happening financially. He has been able to sway the opinions of many people, including ourselves since we started to follow him. During the bailout of Detroit auto manufacturers in 2008/2009 he was able to help people see a distinct difference between Ford and GM and Chrysler. He pointed out that they are very much different corporations, in terms of management structure and approach to environmentalism. Ford has done a good job of introducing new vehicle releases online and through word of mouth before the TV ads even hit the networks.

You Don't Need the Whole World to Agree With You

If you sound like everyone else online you won't have any followers. Creating a following, a group of people with similar values, beliefs, or interests, and motivating them to take action, necessitates us drawing line in the sand, and proclaiming a position.

Doing this may even trim down the number of followers we have at times, but it will help build a much more powerful network of advocates and clients around us. We don't want to dilute our brand or get off message with our own negative conversations or opinions. Being negative can garner attention, but instead focus on creating a vibrant community by contributing to positive conversations, and you will gain a solid reputation.

Don't Be "That Guy"

Of course, please don't be a troll. Some people may not be happy to see their competitor already occupying a solid position in the social media space, and doing well. So they try to shoot holes in the competition's brand, focusing on taking someone else down instead of building themselves up. This is something we see social media newbies do often. This kind of behavior is very obvious and insults the intelligence of those in the community. Secondly, you can't be effective if you have two goals. You should decide whether you are going to get ahead by slandering your competitors or by building a following of your own.

Getting negative, spreading partial truth or celebrating someone else's demise may feel good in the short term, but in time is going to hurt your business. We must go back to your core goal, which is to create a powerful Socialble! brand. This happens from adding to a community, not taking from it.

A bankable *Sociable!* brand is created by truly adding value, engaging people, contributing to community and building people up.

Sometimes, is not just about the truth. When you engage someone, be sure that you are well grounded in your position. If you are making a comment, first consider whether it is a factual statement or just your opinion, and present it as such. Be careful to separate strong opinion from fact, and that can be difficult to do, especially if you're passionate about the topic at hand. If we don't have our facts nailed down, it's actually going to damage your reputation more by making unsubstantiated comments or criticisms. Always ask yourself, "Is it worth saying, and is it my place to say it?"

Chapter Eleven

Your Wake-up Call, Taking it Offline

Once we build a large following using social media, we have to find a way to transition these relationships offline, to the real world, to continue making meaningful connections with people. The key to using social media is taking these relationships and getting them to produce business.

We have seen many people gloat about having thousands of Twitter followers and blog readers and receive kudos from "social media experts." You can hear other people boast that they have 2000 LinkedIn connections or 5000 Facebook friends. Many of those people still struggle to monetize or profit from all of their social media activity.

You need to meet your connections toe-to-toe if you are going to be able to start closing that business. If you're separated by hundreds or thousands of miles you may end up using a webinar or a video conferencing tool to create something as close as possible to meeting in person.

For most of us in most industries that are reading this book right now, you still need to close a deal offline, whether you are selling a car, selling a house, selling your insurance package, your investment advice, selling consulting, selling your next travel cruise somewhere, or even in selling an IT project you have to take it offline. As a minimum you have to get on the phone (or Skype) or get in person and connect.

How Meetup.com Helps Us Get Real

Meetup.com helps people who are engaged in online networking get offline and meet others of similar interest. It creates that all-important personal contact.

Meetup.com has built a solid turnkey system for organizing and promoting events. We have found that connecting with people in real life has accelerated or increased our return on time and energy invested in social media marketing activities.

If your event is properly structured, your people will know who is organizing and hosting. You won't have to over-promote or market to people at your events if you are seen as a thought leader and trusted advisor. You might place a logo here and there, but there is no real sales effort to close deals. Attendees will see you in a positive light. You are no longer just a supplier, you are now also an educational provider.

People who attend and find value in your event may well go back online to Twitter or their blogs, telling everybody about their positive experience. Some people will even write live blogs, broadcasting throughout the event. You will find the online reputation of your events will start to spread like wildfire from that initial group.

Meetups present an opportunity to invite some of your contacts who may be hesitant to try online networking to a more familiar "live" event. They will often pick up on the energy of the occasion, and after learning that most attendees came via social networking invitations, may open up to the idea of connecting online as well.

The Mother of All Meetups

In December 2008, we approached Tanya Davis and Monica Hamburg, organizers of Vancouver's "Third Tuesday Meetup," a group that caters to PR and marketing professionals. The idea was to combine our Real Estate Technology Meetup and Sales Performance Meetup with their Third Tuesday Meetup to create the "Meetup of All Meetups." We discussed combining multiple groups semi-annually so that we could help the organizers expand their influence, and help members make new connections outside of their network and industry. We hosted at a local pub, and combined it with a food drive for the local food bank. Admission was by a donation of canned food goods or money. This added a greater purpose to the occasion. The day of the event, Vancouver was hit with a rare big snowstorm, but to our surprise we still had almost 200 people attend, and everyone raved about the new connections they made and the fun they had.

The real gem in this story is that too often people build fences around their network. Tanya and Monica took a risk by opening up their audience to us, but it helped grow all of three groups, and helped our respective communities. Do be discerning when partnering, though. Your groups should share similar values and social etiquette if it is going to benefit everyone.

The following June we collaborated with seven groups to present another Meetup of all Meetups, this time pushing our venue to capacity with over 450 people attending from seven different Meetup groups. The positive community momentum that has been built has grown our networks and created business opportunities for dozens of people involved.

Other Event Organizing Tools

You don't have to use Meetup.com. There are many other organizational tools. You can use EventBright for events where you need to sell tickets. Evite.com provides an opportunity to send out and track invitations. Both these tools lack the social networking or group building aspect that makes Meetup.com powerful, but they are effective for one-time events.

Facebook and LinkedIn also have built in event promotion and organizing tools. We have found that both lack the ability, thus far, to seamlessly take online payment and registration without using a 3rd party service.

What the Heck is a Tweetup?

Tweetups are a great way for people connected on Twitter to meet in person. While a Meetup tends to be organized by one person, a Tweetup can be an instantaneous event, where several people in a given community decide to meet offline and announce it to the rest of the community. Word spreads in a viral fashion, from one group of followers to another.

There are themed Tweetups, business Tweetups, though many times they are general in nature, sometimes based only on geographic proximity of attendees. Some Tweetups are designed for more social purposes and are focused on people with similar interests such as hiking or fine art. We have thrown some social media specific Tweetups where those who are interested in the topic meet casually, sharing ideas and perhaps a few cocktails as well.

N ISE TO SIGNAL
RobCottingham.ca

Tweetup

LinkedIn-up

A Tweetup can be almost like a web instigated flash mob. Post information about your Tweetup at a given location and next thing you know you might find yourself surrounded by some of your followers. The first time we did it was almost by accident. Yam De La Pena (@tyamdm) posted a Tweet saying, "Hey, I am at Doolin's

Irish Pub with @shanegibson." David Miller (@tastingvan) responded saying, "Hey are you guys having a Tweetup?" We didn't yet know what that was or if we were allowed to have one, but said, "Let's do it." Somebody else posted it as a "Vancouver Tweetup," and within minutes we had 20 people from various industries show up. In less than an hour, people were networking and some are now doing business together. All of this came off with just a quick message to the network saying, "Here I am. Come by if you like."

Leverage your network into other people's Events

Most people should be using Twitter, Facebook, LinkedIn or Meetup to promote their own offline seminars and events as part of their overall marketing plan. If you are going to someone's function, post an update about it on your social networks and your blog to let your groups know you are going to be there. You might pull a few of your own followers along with you who may not have attended otherwise. You get to visit with them in person, and your host will appreciate the extra numbers too.

Social Action Using Twitter

If social media can be used effectively for business improvement, why not apply it to social causes? Vancouver normally has mild winters, but during an uncommon and particularly cold and long lasting winter snowstorm, two local businesspeople recognized a need for their help. Yam De La Pena and Janice Laing spontaneously organized an event they called the TweetupHeatup. They invited people to bring warm coats for the many homeless people living on the streets of Vancouver's downtown east side.

Some 20 people showed up to make a donation, including local newspaper reporter Gillian Shaw, and dozens of people were clothed as a result. Afterwards, Gillian wrote an article in the Vancouver Sun about this impromptu, but much needed charity, and the effectiveness of using social media channels to bring it about. Many other people worldwide heard about the event via Twitter. Some of these people have followed the example, launching similar spontaneous charity events in their own communities. The public profiles of Yam and Janice were substantially boosted, as local readers of the Vancouver Sun saw the article, and the two found themselves communicating with new contacts around the world, reaching them via Twitter.

Guerrilla Tweetups

You can sometimes use a bigger competitor's efforts to your advantage. Some may question this strategy, but if you have few resources or are out gunned economically by large competitors, you have to think like a guerrilla to win.

> *"It's a jungle out there! You are surrounded. All around you are enemies vying for the same bounty… they can't outspend you in areas that money can't buy… [and] they can't always out-think you"* – **Jay and Jeannie Levinson** from *The Startup Guide to Guerrilla Marketing*

Guerilla Tweetups are another way to take it offline, and generate lots of new connections. You do this by leveraging other people's traditional marketing networking and events. Let's say you want to do more business in Chicago. You might find a conference that's going to be there in a few months. You would like to attend but you don't want to pay $20,000 for a booth or you can't get on the speaker roster, but you know there will be good connections in attendance.

A couple of months or so before the conference, you start following people from Chicago on Twitter and begin conversations with people in your target market. If the conference has a LinkedIn page, Facebook page, or blog, join those as well and begin to connect with other attendees and speakers. Book a large hotel suite near the conference venue or, even better, a pub down the street that's willing to give you the space for free for the crowd you're about to bring in to drink beer and eat food. Then you throw an unofficial conference Tweetup sponsored by your company. If you buy the first round of beer, and that's all it usually takes to get a few conference attendees to show up, you can make a lot of new connections without going down the more traditional and expensive route to get to a conference or tradeshow.

We have seen as many as a 100 people show up to a guerilla Tweetup. We have seen numerous entrepreneurs do extremely well using this idea, making good connections, sometimes lifelong business connections, from this type of Guerrilla Tweetup activity.

An added benefit is that when everybody returns home after the conference, you rarely hear people talk about how awesome some booth was, or how exciting it was to hang out in the plenary session. You definitely hear about the Google party or Zappos party that happened outside the main conference. Zappos is famous for holding these types of impromptu Meetups or Tweetups, taking advantage of their home office in Las Vegas, where many conferences and tradeshows are held.

Great Events Have Some Common Elements

An "Educational Event" is a rather loose term. Too many people market their event as educational, but instead end up pushing their product and going for the hard close. This is quite unpleasant for most people. It's a marketing ambush, and is not going to get people to come back time and time again.

You would do better to bring in a speaker who's actually going to benefit your attendees. If you run a car dealership and you are going to bring in a speaker for your clients, don't have your mechanics talk about the great new engine, that's boring product promotion. Have a racecar driver show up and give tips on taking turns, braking technique, or driving in the rain or the snow. That has mass appeal and people will come back the next time you invite them. When it comes time to buy a car, they are more likely to remember and be loyal to the dealership that has been educating them.

Broadcast Your Offline Events Online for Double Leverage

What if your audience is scattered across your country or around the globe, and cannot attend your functions? There are tools available to bring the event to them. You can broadcast events in a number of ways, using a streaming video service. You can also have someone "live blog" or upload pictures to a photo sharing website while the event is happening. We will often interview participants, sharing their perspectives with others who weren't able to engage in conversation during the event.

People like to share their experiences, and they will share their time at your event on their own social networks. By doing so, they promote you and your offerings, and further the range of your exposure. Word of mouth, plus words, pictures and videos on a screen, are great ways to expand your reach. The broad goal is to have a strong and dominant mindshare in the marketplace over your competitors. We do this by contributing and building community. We need to have a strong online reputation integrated with our offline reputation. These strategies will complement and reinforce each other.

From Intellectual to the Street

Blogging, collecting followers, and being on Twitter can all be seen as an intellectual exercise until you begin to show a return on investment. The return doesn't have to be monetary, but it at least must show a strengthening brand, network, or growing community. By taking it offline and getting real, you multiply the return on your investment. You're taking the strategy to the street where the action is.

Chapter Twelve

Owning Your Brand – Online Reputation Management

Social media comprise websites and virtual networks where the majority of the content is user generated content. Twitter owns the website Twitter.com, but the content is created by the users of the site. You may have your own blog, but a lot of content will be reader generated in the form of reader comments. YouTube, with its billion searches per day is all user generated video content.

This content is often opinions or thoughts published. In some cases these will be about your industry, company, or brand. Users in your community are affecting and positioning your brand, your company, your products and your industry through their conversations and the content they create.

If they're raving about your product then you probably want to make sure they share that with as many people as possible. If they're negative, complaining or criticizing you, you're going to want to deal with that before it spins out of control.

You want to know what your customers, prospects and competitors are talking about, and online is a good place to find out. What are your customers' core challenges? What events are they attending? What are their preferences and latest activities? A lot of these questions can be answered through listening in on the right channels.

The First Step in Brand and Reputation Management is Listening

To do this effectively, you cannot just leap in to the social media milieu, you must first develop a social media listening strategy. To begin, monitoring those conversations is critical so that you are aware of what is being said. "Social Search" and other analytics tools for listening number in the hundreds and more are popping up everyday. We present below a few free or low-cost social media monitoring tools available today, recognizing that tomorrow this list will change.

Social Media Monitoring Tools

Google Alerts	google.com/alerts
Google Link Tracking	google.com
Google Blog Search	blogsearch.google.com
Twitter Search	search.twitter.com
Facebook Groups and Pages	Facebook.com
LinkedIn Answers	LinkedIn.com
Yahoo Answers	answers.yahoo.com
Social Mention	socialmention.com
TweetLater	TweetLater.com
BackType	backtype.com
Twitority	Twitority.com
Collecta	collecta.com

We don't use all of these. Most businesses will be able to use Twitter Search, Google Alerts and a service like Social Mention, and have more than enough business intelligence to work with. It comes down to what kind of user interface you prefer, and how the utilities integrate with your business goals and market.

Google Alerts

Let's talk a little about how Google Alerts works. Google "crawls" millions of web pages per day and any new instance where a user-defined key term is mentioned on a webpage, blog, press release or in the news, Google emails you an alert and a link to the where you can find the mention. Imagine you are a manager of a Nobu restaurant in New York, the chain owned by Robert De Niro. You regularly have food bloggers coming in with their smart phones, taking pictures, uploading them to their blogs, or sites such as Urbanspoon.com, and writing reviews about your restaurant. Here you have patrons, often as self-proclaimed food critics, who have thousands of people visiting their websites everyday, and they could be running wild with your brand. When people google your restaurant, they will find reviews from all sorts of "critics" as they decide whether to visit your establishment. Until you begin to monitor these conversations, you won't even know they are happening. And you certainly cannot have any control over what is going on if you're not engaging your fans online.

Google Alerts lets you search the term "Nobu" and your specific address, or maybe just "New York", so that whenever Google finds this written on a new web page, it will email you a link to the page and the time it was updated. You can now visit that blog, see if it is a great new review or not. Naturally, you'd be happy to receive an upbeat review, and would gladly send a note of thanks for one. You might comment on the blog saying, "Thanks for your review. By the way we have some specials coming up and I would love you to come back and check them out," with a link back to your special events. Or you may choose to engage them personally, sending them a quick email to say thanks. This can go a long way to creating loyal customers.

A negative review provides an opportunity to elevate your stature. Fuming privately will earn you no points with anyone. A pessimistic review can indeed be harmful, but if turned into an engaging conversation, you have the potential to win them over. Do it openly and you access their audience, too. You might email them a coupon to encourage their return, inviting them to ask for you personally. This gives you an opportunity to bring a negative reviewer back on side. Engaging a potentially harmful review and addressing criticisms resonates with audiences, demonstrating that you are truly interested in their experiences and perceptions. As you interact, you will be seen as a member of the community, as being more approachable and less likely to have negative news run amuck. It will also help you capitalize on positive comments made about your organization to enhance your branding. Unless you are using a tool like Google Alerts, you won't even know this activity is going on.

Google Link Tracking and Blog Search

There is a function in Google where you type in link:yourdomain.com and it will tell you who is linking to your website. Some of these links will come from social media sites, blogs or other websites or articles. You should be monitoring this as well.

Google Blog Search also does this but only outlines the blogs that are linking to your site. Look at these regularly to see which new websites are talking about you and linking to you so that you can enter into a dialogue with them. You can also use the site blogsearch.google.com to find out what is being said about you on blogs across the web by searching for key terms. This can be organized by date or the authority or popularity of the blogs being searched.

Twitter Search

Search.twitter.com is one of the most timely search tools on the web. While a search on Google will tell you what has been said, searching Twitter tells you what is *being said right now*. It provides immediate access to current conversations going on about your brand or another specific topic of interest. It returns results of comments on Twitter, as they occur. You can only get involved in the conversation if you know that it is happening.

Keying in search terms like "pub near:Chicago" or "dining out near:LA" will give you updates only in that geographical region. If you are a pub owner in Chicago, you could benefit greatly knowing what these conversations are. You can begin to follow people who are talking about your sector, like-minded people, those that value what you do or what you stand for.

Twitter's advanced search (search.twitter.com/advanced) can help you focus your search within specific geographic areas as well as time frames and even between specific people. Combined with the keyword search this can quickly tell you what is being said about a topic or between two people.

You should also consider searching out comments about your competition. You may able to convert a competitor's disgruntled clients just by engaging them while they are making complaints on Twitter.

Twitority

Twitority.com is a Twitter search tool that uses data from Twitter's search engine but lets you sort the search results according to the authority (number of followers) that people have. This way you will get the results from those who have a potentially higher influence. It helps filter out people who may not have a lot of influence but makes a lot of noise by frequently updating.

Tweetlater

You can set up TweetLater to do what Google Alerts does, but returning results from the Twitter stream for any key terms you want to monitor. It automates the activity of keeping up to date on key conversations on Twitter about you, your brand, your products and competitors, so that you won't need to go to search.twitter.com all the time.

Yahoo! Answers, LinkedIn Answers, and Facebook

You should be searching these networks to see who is talking about your business, communicating about you, your products, brand, or competitors.

LinkedIn and Yahoo have built in search functions that allow you to monitor conversations on their question and answer forums. You can also join specific groups or discussions and opt to have email alerts sent to you as new information is posted or in some cases when certain keywords are mentioned.

Facebook groups and pages require a more manual type of monitoring. Find groups and pages where your target market, existing customers and competitors are. Scan the conversations and topics for opportunities to connect with your target market.

BackType Comment Search

Most blog search sites like Technorati or Google omit the results from comments made on blog posts. Comments are a big part of the social media conversation and branding that occurs. A great tool to track this conversation is BackType. The front page of their website says it best, BackType allows you to:

1. Claim and share your comments:
   Claim the comments you write on blogs, social networks and other social media

2. Subscribe to search results:
   Receive updates whenever a search term is mentioned in a comment

3. Connect conversations:
   View all the conversations related to a specific article or post

4. Subscribe to conversations:
   Receive updates whenever a conversation you're following becomes active

By signing up for their service you "give your comments a home where they can be discovered, followed and shared."

Even if you don't sign up, you can use their search box to find the comments you are looking for and you can subscribe to them via RSS as well. Once you set up the searches you want to monitor, they can be delivered to your feed reader on a minute-by-minute basis as the conversation and comments evolve.

BackType also has a spin off service called Backtweets. com that shows you everyone who is tweeting about a specific website. This is a great tool to find people that are talking about your site or a site of interest to you on Twitter.

Collecta and Social Mention

Collecta and Social Mention pull all of the aforementioned search tools into one. You can search just microblogs, video sites, blogs, or search every social site type at once. Social Mention even rates the positive versus negative comments and a number of other "reputation metrics" for you. These tools are great but depending on your agenda and what you are listening for, they may be overkill.

You Are Listening, but Now What?

Now comes the time to apply the engagement skills you have learned in this book. When you observe a conversation about you, your company or your brand, get *Sociable!* On Twitter this could mean commenting on something said or inviting them to your blog to see a personal response to their conversation. It may be inviting them out to an event or into your store or showroom if appropriate.

If it's a comment or topic of interest on their blog or video channel, get involved in the conversation, adding value and displaying thought leadership if at all possible. The conversations and comments that show up in social media searches are openings, they are opportunities to add value and get permission to begin a relationship with your prospects, customers and community.

Chapter Thirteen

Implementing Social Media and Social Networking in Your Organization

The brilliance in any social media social networking plan is in the implementation. There are several important steps to consider when implementing a social media strategy. If you are a team of one, this can be a bit more intuitive, maybe a bit less structured, but it is still important for you to consider these core steps to make sure that you have a process nailed down. As your social media presence develops, these steps are going to be important to helping you manage this growth.

Everyone Needs to Know the Rules of Engagement

The first step in getting involved in social media, whether you are an individual or leading a large corporate team, is making sure that everyone understands the rules of engagement. This equates to getting training on the principles of social media engagement and thought leadership. While the tools you use will change, as will the conversations and the environments in which they occur, the principles are going to stay relatively the same.

Have a Social Media Policy and Guidelines

The second step is implementing your social media policy. Following are the social media policy and guidelines that we developed for ourselves and those that may work with us or represent the Sociable! brand. It lays out the core steps that we have to follow in order to protect and grow the Sociable! brand and to make sure we are acting in the spirit of positive engagement and thought leadership.

The *Sociable!* Code of Engagement

#1) Treat every action as if it will be recorded for eternity.

Almost everything we say online is recorded, logged and backed up somewhere. In every restaurant, bar or conference room, there are dozens of people with mobile video, photo, and blogging apps that can capture our behavior, ready to broadcast it to the world instantly and permanently. You can't delete a bad blog post, a rude response. Be careful of what you say, blog, tweet and do, because the impact can be permanent.

#2) Talk about what you know.

Being *Sociable!* is about being a thought leader, and contributor to community, and being authentic and transparent. People rely on us for advice and guidance. Stating opinion as fact can hurt our reputation, and it may even harm the person taking our advice. If you're wrong about something, you can expect to be called out on it and possibly embarrassed in the social media space by other bloggers or community members. Always be learning, studying and fact checking in the domains you aspire to lead, and don't exaggerate or fabricate your knowledge or facts.

#3) Get Engaged.

Don't broadcast, connect. Being *Sociable!* is about listening, connecting, and contributing. Engagement is about how we make other people feeland the lasting impact that we have on them and their success. To be Sociable! you must monitor conversations, listening to and communicating with individuals in the community in a personable and relevant way.

#4) Digital Rights and Giving Credit Where Credit Is Due

If you hear a great quote from someone, an interesting hypothesis or learn a new business process, make sure you give the author due credit. Just because something is not protected under copyright does not mean we can re-purpose it without giving credit. A link back to their site, a mention of them at your seminar or in your video only takes seconds. This builds the trust of everyone watching you, and they will know you're in this for more than just personal gain. And they will be *Sociable!* with you as well.

We make our living from the great ideas, content and creative works we create, market and produce. Being *Sociable!* means our brand is one of integrity, authenticity and transparency. We need to respect others copyright and creative works just like we would want them to do for us. Always ask permission or give attribution to other people's creations that you use, cite, or include in your work. Every photo, video, quote or audio clip we use must be posted and distributed in a way that respects and maintains the integrity of their work.

#5) No Spam

Never send generic messages to people who have given you permission to connect. If they have added you as a connection in a social network, realize that this is not to be taken lightly. Only send information or communicate in a way that is adding value. Avoid auto messages, auto blog links, or auto anything that makes people feel like a number and not a valued contact.

#6) Know When to Zip it

Be conscious of private or confidential information that has been trusted to you. This means don't post it anywhere on the web. It also means don't talk about it in public, where someone else could hear or record you and post it online for the world to see. Know the difference between fact, opinion and slander and always err on the side of being legally diligent. In other words, don't post anything that could result in an unwanted court appearance.

#7) This is Not a Video Game

Some people see social media as a video game where you collect names and followers, to be presented in some sort of digital trophy case. This game is getting old fast. The real measure of someone who is legitimately *Sociable!* is their action and impact. Focus on the quality of relationships with people. Focus on getting people to do something when they get to your blog, not on how many people visit it. Think in the term of profits made, impact created or actions caused by your Sociable! activity.

#8) Be Open to All Feedback

The days of corporate white washing are over, so is having a dual life. Everyone now knows what you're up to in this digital world that lacks privacy. If, or when, you make mistakes, people are going to go after you online on your personal blog, your corporate blog or blast you with a video or a comment on a social network. When this happens, don't hide and don't delete their comments or errors you may have made. Instead, engage. Customer complaints are branding opportunities and sometimes our critics are actually bold allies trying to set us straight. It's important to respond to criticism strategically, not emotionally, and to set the record straight with a correction, the facts, or good old fashion customer service and apologies.

#9) Be *Sociable!*

Being *Sociable!* also means not taking our self or our brand too seriously. In order to be a true Sociable! thought leader we must have fun, be passionate and contribute to the success of our clients, peers, family and community as a whole. Most importantly, we continually strive to "get real" by taking our online connections and meet them individually or as a community through events like

Meetups, Tweetups, and community functions. We do this to deepen and expand relationships. Without strong *Sociable!* relationships we're just another marketer or salesperson making a pitch.

After the Rules Of Engagement Come Training in the Tools of Engagement

Whether you work in a large corporation or have only five staff, we believe it is important that you put together a training program, or find a qualified outsource partner to deliver social media training. A one on one internal mentoring program can also work.

Give training on the basics of how to set up a Facebook or Twitter account, or perhaps how to create and maintain a blog. Teach basic skills, such as how to put a video blog up on YouTube or Viddler. These are pretty straight forward things and most of these resources are available online. All you may need to do is have a central wiki or blog page on your intranet that links to external training resources so that people know where to get the information on how to do it. You may want to ask for help from the most socially and technologically aware person on your team to develop a basic training course.

Make sure that your people actually take action. Getting involved is often easier than most people expect, but they just don't know where to start. The purpose of training is to familiarize them enough to take away fear and give them a place to start.

If you don't have the internal resources or confidence to build your own training program, you can outsource to an organization specializing in training individuals and companies on how to effectively implement these tools. Marketingprofs.com is a great resource for the principles of engagement using these tools, and you can either take individual webinars or buy a one-year membership that gives you unlimited access to hundreds of training programs.

Keep it Professional

Provide guidance as to what is appropriate to say online, and what is inappropriate. For a funky running shoe company that caters to club kids, posting the term #shitshow in their Twitter stream or on the company blog is probably okay. If you work at a bank, it's probably not advisable. As we discussed in the chapter on social media etiquette, there are different social norms for different platforms and demographic groups. Your social media policy and strategy needs to address this.

Dealing with departing employees

One of the questions we get asked all the time is if an employee quits and have a thousand followers on their Twitter account, should they have to hand it over when they leave? If it's their personal name or brand, they should be able to take their network with them, but for a period of time should post information letting their followers know how to get in touch with other people in the company. If they are operating an account such as a blog, a Twitter profile, a Facebook page, or a Meetup with your brand attached to it, then they must hand it over. It's brand specific social capital that you have paid them to build for you. You need policies in place in regards to how you are going to deal with these issues well in advance. You may want to decide as a team, since agreeing on corporate policy can make implementation easier and more productive.

Motivate and reward

Feeling micro-managed is not conducive to fostering creativity or being sociable. Have a clear policy that describes appropriate sociable behavior, then reward suitable creativity or boldness. Social media success is often achieved through pushing limits, by taking bold and creative actions. Your policy needs to protect your brand but it also needs to promote innovation and creativity.

Your Policy Needs to Be Human not Marketing Focused

Allow your staff to inject some of their own personality into their social media efforts. They are people, and we interact socially with people, not the blogs they produce. The blog is just the medium. By permitting employees to be themselves online, their character and interests can attract followers to their social media accounts, and therefore to your brand, who you may not have reached otherwise.

Each employee can have their own followers based on what they do within the business and based on what they are up to in their personal time.

The point is to humanize your business, because we want to be *Sociable!* with humans, not a business. Your existing client base in your target market is going to make up a large percentage of your online connections, but the idea with social media networking is that it allows you to cast your net broader and deeper than you could traditionally.

It's a Leadership Issue

Note From Shane Gibson: We have learned a number of great lessons about the implementation of new business practices through our consulting work at Knowledge Brokers International. We have put into service large-scale sales performance pro-grams for organizations like ABSA bank in South Africa, BMW, Siemens, the Certified Management Accountants of Canada, and a multitude of other organizations across four continents.

We have realized is that there isn't a common-ality dictated by industry or by company size as to who is better in implementing a new method of doing business. We have found that organiza-tions with strong leadership are typically the most successful in executing change. It is not the best technological advantage, it is not the age of the company, it is not the brand, it is the organization with the strongest leadership. The leadership must both guide and reinforce change.

You can have an employee manual, a social media busi-ness plan and policy, and all the training in the world, but without strong mentoring along with a method of mea-surement and a level of accountability it is unlikely this change is going to stick.

Some people in your organization will naturally take to engaging in social media, but there will be others who are going to need some guidance, some hand holding, and positive reinforcement.

Not everybody in an organization should be forced to get involved in social media, but those that agree to use it as a tool have to be accountable to follow through on that goal. This is not a test, it is a commitment. Introducing any new process is not going to meet with success if its implementation is not mandatory, whether it is a change in sales procedure, adaptation of a new technological tool, or a new way of answering the telephone.

Your Strategy Must Support the Flattening of Your Organization

When you undertake a social media strategy, you are also expanding your marketing department to encompass everyone using social media. And the more people on your *Sociable!* team, the stronger you can be. Ideally, you want your customer service people answering questions through Facebook or Twitter, and hopefully you will see your marketing people doing the marketing, and sales people prospecting and networking using social media. Social media should not be about one department of a business, it impacts all parts of a business and that is why all departments should be involved.

The tone that the CEO and vice presidents establish online and in the office often sets the precedent and pace for adopting social media policies and strategies. The CEOs of Zappos, BuildDirect, and ING Direct all take leadership roles in finding their voice and using it in social media. There is a necessary leadership element in implementing your plan to grow a Sociable! company.

Please Facebook at Work!

Saying that you don't want to use social media at the office to engage clients is a non-starter. We believe you have to do it. We believe it is a lot like saying years ago, "I don't want to talk to customers on the phone," or 10 years ago "I don't want to interact with customers online." It is not an option for a business with a desire to grow. If you are in customer service, sales and marketing, or management, it is your obligation to engage customers, to get out to the community and grow your brand.

We believe that organizations making social media and social networking an intrinsic part of job descriptions and corporate agendas are those ones that are going to succeed. Senior management at BuildDirect.com had this view when they sent out this email on the following page:

From: "Rob Jones" <robjones@builddirect.com>
To: "All Build Direct Staff"
Date: Thu, 16 Oct 2008 12:38:52 -0800
Subject: Please Facebook While at Work

That's right, people – please use Facebook while at work. Sales, logistics, finance, IT – we want you.

What I mean to say is that we've set up a BuildDirect company page on Facebook as a means of creating a community for all employees (that's you), your friends, and your favorite customers, vendors, suppliers. And we want you to contribute to it, and share in its growth.

We want you to share your content, your thoughts, and your stories on "the wall". If you've got links to videos of personal DIY projects or even videos not entirely related to our business, images, notes, links to sites, etc – anything you think would be of interest to customers who are looking to find out who they're doing business with when they come to the **BuildDirect** *site, then it's fair game on our page. Try to avoid salesy 'have I got a deal for you' stuff, like any other social networking forum of course. Otherwise, we want you to have some fun with this (G rated fun, obviously).*

I want to underline a point; this is not a marketing page. ***This is a BuildDirect page.***

This means that it belongs to you once you become a fan. *No matter what department you're in, we want to hear from you. And if you have direct contact with favorite customers, suppliers, vendors, whoever – invite them to join too. The best way to gain trust with customers and other day-to-day contacts is to let them know that we're not just a site on the internet – we're a bunch of people just like they are.*

So, I invite you to please use Facebook at work – and participate in your page!

Sociable!

Cheers,

RJ.

Rob Jones
Marketing Coordinator

BuildDirect *1900-570 Granville St. Vancouver, BC, V6C 3P1 Canada*

Tel 778 331 1146   *Toll Free Phone 1 877 631-2845*
Fax (604)662-8142   *Toll Free Fax 1 877 664-2845*

www.builddirect.com

This is the type of bold community building engagement that makes it easy for a company like BuildDirect to stimulate creativity, community building and staff morale.

Your Social Media Strategy

After your policy is established there are a few key issues that need to be addressed in your strategy:

1. Identify Your Goal
2. Identify Your Target Audience
3. Pick the Right Platforms
4. Map out Social Etiquette
5. Implement Listening Strategy
6. Know Core Pains
7. Uniquely Communicate Solutions Mixing Marketing and Community

Indentifying Your Goals

Deciding to get on Facebook because Shane and Stephen said you should is a bad idea. Blogging just because your competitors are doing it is equally weak in its strategic significance. Here are some good examples of annual goals:

- ✓ To be the number one trusted resource for information on the green building supply industry in our target markets.
- ✓ To increase Army recruitment by 5% this year through engaging 18 to 23 year old men and women through interactive blogs, community driven video content and Twitter.
- ✓ To reduce marketing costs by 90% by ceasing all print advertising and focusing on blogging, YouTube, Facebook, and Twitter to market my real estate developments.
- ✓ To land 10 new conference clients by building an online community for event planners and engaging them using video, forums, blog entries and monthly webcasts.

You need a solid goal. In project management they are called SMART goals.

S: Specific
Your goal needs to be very specific about who you are targeting down to at least 5 to 7 core measurable attributes like geography, industry, income level, size of company, stage of business growth, gender etc.

M: Measurable
Decide how you are going to measure your ROI. Increased website visitors? Revenues? Employee morale? Acquiring business intelligence? Amount of profit?

A: Achievable

Based upon my resources or resourcefulness, is this specific goal achievable? Better yet, what has to happen in order for this to be achievable?

R: Realistic

With the present resources and specific goals I have set, is this a realistic goal?

T: Timely

Your goal must have a specific time line. Napoleon Hill once said, "There are no unrealistic goals only unrealistic time lines." You may need to extend or shrink your deadline based upon the goal, but without a time limit we often will have no sense of urgency to complete our plan.

Identify Your Target Audience

We have all heard of the 80/20 rule. KBI developed a series of weighted criteria and questions to help clients identify the 20% of customers that will bring 80% of their business. When developing your strategy for social media engagement and marketing there are several 20% type vertical markets or target markets you need to focus on.

The most obvious person you will want to connect with and influence is the decision maker. This is an easy target to aim for. But the person deciding to purchase your product or service is not necessarily the one to use it.

The second group you want to pursue is the end user. While they may not have the ultimate decision making power, they can most certainly have an impact on the choices made by those who do. So you need to be educating and conversing with them. Whereas traditional marketing and sales channels may have had little contact with many, if any, end users in some markets, your social media efforts will provide you with more access than you've ever had with this crowd. You can position your brand with those who use it, and don't discount their level of potential influence. These key people also network with peers their industry and can pass on your message through positive conversations.

You should broaden your target audience to a still wider group, however. With social media, your reach can go much further than your existing and identified intended clients. If your content is sufficiently fantastic, or if you're just lucky, you may see your message go viral, passed on by others to amplify and multiply your efforts. You may have many loyal blog readers, maybe a Facebook group and a Twitter crowd as well, but that's a small part of the massive audience available on the internet. You need to develop criteria that help you hone and deliver your message to the thought leaders who can ideally pass it on to their own audiences and communities.

Note From Shane Gibson: My target client companies when I am selling sales training and sales systems do at least $50 million per year in revenues, have at least 20 dedicated large account sales people in the team, are in regions I work in, and are usually in financial services, manufacturing, or the high tech sector.

The end users are the sales people that get trained by our team. We need to be a household name to them. The person who cuts the check and gives the green light is usually the CEO or the VP of sales.

Thought leaders that influence these two groups online are usually other authors, speakers, trainers, or consultants who cater to the same target market as we do. From a blogging perspective here is how I would reach out to all of these groups:

Blog entry #1 would describe how to build a strong sales and leadership culture in your organization with in-depth statistics to back it up. This appeals to the senior executive.

Blog entry #2 would provide 10 ways to generate leads without cold calling, with a list of portals and communities where salespeople can find warm leads. This appeals to the sales people.

Blog entry #3 would be on "Why Every Company Needs to Invest in Sales Training." I may link to or quote well known sales thought leaders in the article. Sometimes these same thought leaders will share the piece with their followers, thereby expanding your reach.

Your social media strategy must specifically identify these major groups. You need to use mediums and messages that are going to appeal to all three if it you intend to drive your business. If you are strictly selling to individuals you will not need to worry about addressing upper management, so you may only be focusing on end users and thought leaders.

Pick the Right Platforms

Once you have set your goal and have identified your target audiences you need to determine which platforms you will need to focus on to engage your target market. Which social networks or groups within those social networks have the highest concentration of end-users, thought leaders, or senior executives?

The Right Platform Now and the Right Platform Later

In early 2008 when we first got on Twitter it was not a great place to engage a CEO or help build a following of Mommy Bloggers. Today it's the perfect tool for that. Be careful in looking at historical data or what is happening right now when choosing your platforms. Instead look at which ones have the biggest opportunity for growth and invest in building your network before the masses rush in.

> **Note From Stephen Jagger:** Realtor bloggers were few and far between when I started Blog. Ubertor.com. In fact a lot of bloggers in the space are doing it as a result of what we were doing at Ubertor. We were blogging a full two years before most real estate professionals posted even a single blog entry. While they are trying to ramp up content and readers we are reaping the benefits of being an early adopter. You have to at least look mid-term if not long-term at most of these tools.

Map Out Social Etiquette

We spent an entire chapter on this topic but lets review it in the context of making it part of your plan. When you choose a platform (Facebook, LinkedIn, Twitter, etc.) each has its own social rules and norms. If you're not sure what they are, connect with and follow someone who is established and observe their habits, conversations and types of content they post overtime. This will dictate to some degree what types of messaging and the level of marketing jargon or promoting you can get away with.

You need to know how conservative or liberal your target market is and how formal and or informal they are. This will determine what kind of messages, videos, and photos you would share on Twitter or Facebook. Lastly, look at cross-cultural implications – is your target market global? If so then what issues do you have to address?

Implement a Listening Strategy

Social Media monitoring, social search, and just plain reading other people's blogs are all part of your listening strategy. In order to be effective at influencing people we must have a high amount of empathy and understanding of them. If we listen intently enough our market will expose pains that need fulfillment and the missing solutions.

Know Core Pains

Hopefully by listening and directly engaging your target markets you will develop a grounded and complete view of what ails them or their business. A 16-year-old teenager may crave knowledge of the most current fashion trends, but for a marketing executive at a Fortune 500 company, their pain may be an inability to measure advertising return on investment. Once we understand these core pains we need to position ourselves or our products and services as a pill to remedy their problems.

Give them the solution through marketing and community

What is your target market typing into Google right now? If you sell Hyundai cars in North Carolina, maybe your target market is looking for "Low interest car loans with no credit history" or "Best new car warranty." Writing a generic blog entry about a Santa Fe or the all new

Elantra isn't going to let that person know your dealership can solve their particular pain. A blog entry on "How to get a low interest car loan with no credit history" or "Who has the best new car warranty of all import manufacturers" is likely going to be spit out in Google for them when they're searching for pills for their pain. Provide answers to those pains when you're on Twitter. Your YouTube videos should also address the same.

Spend some time brainstorming the top ten pains that each of your target markets have, then create a blogging, Twitter, YouTube, and/or Facebook strategy to give them the solutions to those pains. Over time this will help position your company and make your brand relevant and top of mind for your target groups.

Conclusion

Sociable! The Road Ahead

People who read this book in an attempt to find the silver bullet for using social media in sales and marketing probably have come to a rude awakening by now. There is no silver bullet. Success principles in business that have been around for several decades still apply to social media marketing.

This book is about applying proven best practices in leadership and authentic selling with new social media tools. Some of the take-aways we have shared include:

Know where you want to go

Set goals, measure, and get real. In business, sales and profit are the ultimate measures of success.

Contribute

The more you contribute and add value the more magnetic you and your brand become.

Be unique

If you sound like everyone else, you're just noise. Find unique ways to market, sell, lead and create content on the web.

Always add value

Social media is 90% adding value, contribution and connection and 10% marketing and sales. Just like a great sales meeting with a client.

Experiment

Some of the world's greatest inventions came out of serendipitous events. Be willing to try new things, new mediums and new ideas.

Be transparent and honest

It's a lot easier to be yourself than to promote a facade. In today's hyper-connected marketplace there's no hiding. Transparency and honesty build trust and long-term revenues.

Embrace change

This is a guiding principle and a key skill. Our ability to adapt and profit from change is more important now than ever before. Regardless of whether or not you're using social media right now, you need to apply these principles to succeed in any business. If you're already doing this offline, it's time to take those skills and apply them in the highly leveraged social media space to make a bigger impact in the marketplace.

Where the title *Sociable!* came from

We had several title ideas for this book that we shared with many people. Some were clever, some were trendy, and some were just downright odd.

We had just finished the first draft of the book and sent it off to our editor. Sitting down in one of the many pubs in Vancouver where we do some of our best marketing strategy sessions, the title just came to us. It was almost accidental. Shane raised a pint of Keith's India Pale Ale, brewed in Nova Scotia, and in celebration of the completion of the first draft (no pun intended), exclaimed "Sociable!" Shane's family is from the east coast of Canada. In Nova Scotia, "Sociable!" is one of the ways to say cheers.

It also means more than "cheers." People will often say "I'm going for a Sociable," referring to heading down to the pub or to a community event to have a few beverages with friends and connect with the community.

The art of the "Sociable!" is our meme. Most of the business we close for speaking, training, or outsourcing clients still happens this way. We believe that people buy from people. When you can get someone out of his or her stuffy office, loosen your ties together, get real and build authentic rapport, great things can happen.

For this reason we chose "Sociable!" as the title of the book. It's all about using technology to connect in a meaningful way. The goal is to initiate the beginning of a real relationship that leads to network growth, profit and fun.

It's our hope that you use the lessons in this book to connect, collaborate, and profit in your sales and marketing endeavors.

We look forward to getting *Sociable!* with you soon.

Steve and Shane
Vancouver, BC
September 30th 2009

About Stephen Jagger

Stephen Jagger is an entrepreneur that has been starting businesses since high school. He is currently involved in 3 businesses. Combustion Labs Media Inc, which operates as Ubertor.com, is a real estate software company that provides websites and online marketing tools to thousands of real estate agents across North America. Reachd. com is a training company that focuses on marketing professionals and businesses that are interested in learning more about search engine optimization, blogging, online video, Google Adwords and social media. The 3rd is OutsourcingThingsDone.com, which provides high level, outsourced personnel to business owners and mangers across North America.

Stephen has been covered in many major publications including The Vancouver Sun, The Wall Street Journal, The Ottawa Citizen, The Vancouver Courier, The Calgary Herald plus many more. He has spoken at many different events including British Columbia Institute of Technology, The Vancouver Board of Trade, The Entrepreneurs' Organization (EO), The Real Estate Board of Greater Vancouver, and Inman News Connect 2007 in San Francisco where he was on a panel of 4 with a representative from Google, Yahoo and the Yellow Pages and 2009 in New York on a panel discussing blogging.

He is very active in the community as a member of the Vancouver Board of Trade Communication Committee, the Vancouver College Alumni Association, a volunteer with Kids Help Phone, the founding member of the largest real estate agent Meetup in North America and a mentor for the Leaders of Tomorrow program.

Stephen can be reached at: stephen.jagger@gmail. com for your speaking requests and business consulting needs. Follow Stephen on Twitter @sjagger. Visit Stephen's blog at Blog.Ubertor.com.

About Shane Gibson

Shane Gibson is an international speaker, and author who has addressed over 100,000 people over the past sixteen years on stages in North America, Southern Africa and South America. He is in high demand as a keynote speaker on the topics of social media and sales performance.

Shane is also President of Knowledge Brokers International North America (KBI). Internationally with offices in Canada, South Africa, and affiliates in Kuwait, KBI has implemented large-scale sales performance programs with SAB Miller, SIEMENS Industry and Transport Division, ACER Computers, Africon Engineering, Old Mutual, BMW, Vodacom, and dozens of major financial services companies on three continents.

As a trainer, coach and speaker Shane combines a diverse background in sales force leadership, new entrepreneur development and social media marketing to develop unique presentations and solutions for his clients.

Blogging since 2002, and podcasting since 2004 Shane drives the majority of his business from social media, and social networks. Shane Gibson is also the author of *Closing Bigger: The Field Guide to Closing Bigger Deals*. He has been published in numerous publications as an authority on the topics of leadership, marketing, social media, and sales performance. Some of these publications include CMA Magazine, the Financial Post, the Globe and Mail and Profit Magazine.

Shane's speaking and training clients that he has worked with include: Ford, CMA Canada, The Vancouver Board of Trade, Ford Motor Company, HUB International, Seminarium Colombia, Seminarium Chile, BuildDirect.com, the Sauder School of Business, the University of British Columbia, Canaccord Financial and hundreds of entrepreneurs, individual sales people and marketers over the past 16 years.

When he's not working or tweeting you can find Shane hiking or skiing in British Columbia's Coast Mountain range with his family.

Shane can be reached at: shane@closingbigger.net or visit ShaneGibson.tel for your speaking requests and business consulting needs. Follow Shane on Twitter @ ShaneGibson. Visit Shane's blog and podcast at Closing-Bigger.net.

For more information on our books, seminars, and training programs visit:

SociableBook.com